51 Alternatives to a Real Job

By
Jason Alba

51 Alternatives to a Real Job

Because of the dynamic nature of the Internet, any Web addresses or links contained in this book may have changed since publication and may no longer be valid. The views expressed in this work are solely those of the author.

ISBN: 978-0-9896186-0-1

Printed in the United States of America

INTRODUCTION

This book took me a couple of years to write. It should have been a two-week project but I sat on it for a long time. I didn't feel right about certain things. When I decided to add quotes from people who are making money with these Alternatives, it became a much bigger project. As I have come back to the manuscript time and again, I tweaked the concept until it became what I wanted to put in your hands.

This is not an exhaustive list of fifty-one things you should do. Some of these Alternatives are not things you would ever actually do. They are too dirty, too hard, or too simple. Some of them would take too long to realize a return. Some won't provide the income you want, or will take you too far outside your comfort zone. I wrote this book to inspire you.

By reading the stories, testimonials and examples, I hope you're motivated to act on your own ideas. After reading 51 Alternatives, I want you to say, "Yes, I can do this! And the time is now!"

Many of these Alternatives will make you enough money to pay your bills. Some Alternatives can be scaled to make millions while others are so labor or time-intensive, they don't scale easily. Though each Alternative provides information about startup costs, legal considerations, local regulations, and possible marketing options, you should perform your own due diligence – research, investigation, and talking with others – to determine whether it will be a good fit for you.

I am a firm believer in generating "multiple streams of income." Businesses use this model. Successful and financially sound people make it their lifestyle. It might make more sense for you to work on three or four Alternatives than to focus on one. Maybe one of your revenue streams is your "day job." That is fine! But don't put yourself in the position where you have only one revenue stream, which is what most people with a job do. Diversify your income so if something happens to one revenue stream, you have others in place, and you don't lose 100 percent of your income.

Starting and running a business is HARD. I remember the few days I spent filling out paperwork for my state business license and business checking account. It was a royal pain. I hate paperwork and stupid bureaucratic forms. I remember wondering why anyone would go into business for themselves if it took so much work to get through the dreary administrative stuff. I soon discovered that was the easy part. There have been highs and lows, and I stretched myself in many ways. Finding money to keep the business alive before revenue came in was a challenge. Getting customers and keeping up with market changes and technology was a challenge. Even in my eighth year of business, I still work through challenges. But I know there would be challenges if a day job was my only income. The dark cloud over everyone with a day job today is the ever-present threat of layoffs. I've obviously chosen the path of an entrepreneur, and continue to stay away from what was once the stable, acceptable, and safe choice.

As you read this book, I want you to be inspired to start something right now. This isn't just a fun book with a list of fifty-one things to read about, and then put away. Let the ideas in this book compel you to act. Even if your first venture doesn't make you money, or grow very large, you haven't failed. What you learn with your first venture will make you stronger and wiser for when you start your second and third ventures. The skills you acquire along the way, and the wisdom you gain as a business owner, will help you make better decisions and be more prepared for your next big thing.

As with all of my projects, I'm nervous about not delivering enough. However insufficient the actual Alternatives might seem, if you are open to becoming more self-empowered, you will draw what you need from the pages here and act. Instead of spending two more years refining, polishing and perfecting this book, I hope you get what you need out of this edition.

That's it. Turn the page and let's get started!

Jason Alba: Entrepreneur and Career Management 3.0 Advocate
www.51Alternatives.com
www.JibberJobber.com
www.JasonAlba.com
www.ImOnLinkedInNowWhat.com

Career Management 3.0

The tagline for JibberJobber has been "Career Management 2.0" since I launched a contest to help me come up with a better tagline than the one I was using. As I started speaking around the country, I delivered a program I called Career Management 2.0, which has been my most popular presentation. After giving that presentation a number of times, I started to wonder what Career Management 3.0 would look like.

I didn't think 3.0 should be the same as 2.0, but more intense or deeper. It should be a radical change. I came up with the following definitions for each of the ideas of career management:

Career Management 1.0 is the old, traditional career where we could count on companies to show some loyalty. Get a degree, work hard, do a good job and retire with a nice pension. That plan is history.

Career Management 2.0 is where we are now. We have to take a lot more responsibility for our career progression and transitions. Networking and personal branding have A LOT to do with this, and they are the crux of my Career Management 2.0 presentation.

Career Management 3.0 is where we introduce multiple revenue streams into our portfolio. Income from a job is just one revenue stream. It might be the largest, but it doesn't have to be the most important. I predict this is where we are headed, and that is why I wrote this book.

51 Alternatives to a Real Job is all about Career Management 3.0. If you naively want to trust your company to provide your income through retirement, go for it. If you want to be more empowered, and less vulnerable to forces outside of your control, start moving towards Career Management 3.0!

FOREWORD

By
Dick Bolles
What Color Is Your Parachute

Lots of people want to go off the beaten path. This most particularly occurs in the world of work. The poet, Robert Frost, captured this human tendency in his poem, The Road Not Taken, with its famous line: "Two roads diverged in a wood, and I – I took the one less traveled by . . . "

People who want to go off the beaten path in the world of work are searching for what are technically called odd jobs. A search of these words on Amazon or other online bookstores will turn up a number of volumes. The search is perennial, but it is particularly acute when times are tough. However, there are problems.

First of all, for some strange reason, people who have odd jobs are often reluctant to admit it. This may be due to other connotations of the word "odd" as in he's rather an odd fellow, don't you think? You can try to tease out odd job people, by some kind of contest with a reward, and still they will not come forward. Odd, isn't it?

Second, people who attempt to list odd jobs often describe just what a person does, without describing what skills are required, what preparation is necessary, and what one may hope to earn at that odd job.

Finally, people who attempt to list odd jobs often have never tried any of them. They speak from a distance.

What makes this little book of Jason Alba's unique is that he has solved all three of these problems. He actually discovered 51 odd jobs, no small accomplishment in view of the eerie silence I mentioned. He describes in detail what it takes to do each odd job. And he has tried some of these jobs, so he can report what that job feels like from the inside.

So if you are considering the road less traveled, full or part-time, you may find real inspiration from reading Jason's well-researched list. Maybe you will even think of some odd job no one else has ever thought of before. I commend this book to you.

Table of Contents

Babysitter

Before we had children, my wife babysat for a family with five kids. Both parents worked while my wife spent the day at their house taking care of their kids. It was easy money for her, and she loved those kids.

Many years later, I lost my job and was unemployed for a few months. My wife began caring for a four-year-old girl in our home every day. This job fits into my wife's schedule wonderfully. When I started writing this book, she learned about another babysitting opportunity for a cute sixteen-month-old boy who was with us almost every workday from seven in the morning until four thirty in the afternoon.

Adding one more buddy into the mix of kids at our house works well. When my wife runs errands she takes all the kids with her. The kids she cares for are immediately accepted by our kids, and for the few hours they are with us, they are a part of our family.

How much can you make doing this? It varies by location. In Utah, the rates for long-term daily babysitting start around three dollars per hour per kid. In Maryland, two children for twenty-four hours can run around $125 to $150. During a dinner in northern California, a fellow diner told me her teen daughter sometimes earns twenty dollars per hour. Prices in some big cities might surprise you. You can charge more for short notice while giving quantity discounts to regular clients or for long blocks of time.

Babysitting isn't for everyone. You have to do it for more than the money. People need to know their children feel loved, are safe, and having a good time. As a parent, those are the top three things I look for in a babysitter. A sitter who provides consistent love, a safe environment and pays attention to the child can do especially well.

You can care for more than one kid, but usually there are laws about how many kids you can watch without (a) being licensed or (b) having more adults to help (often referred to as the "kid-to-adult" ratio). Check with your municipal or state office for local requirements.

Pricing can be competitive. My wife explains, "I like the flexibility of charging a little less than the going rate. It allows room to live your life how you want with your own children and provide a nice home and family environment for the child you are tending as you plug them into what you are already doing." Charging a little less can be the key to getting the job.

INSPIRED BY: My wife, Kaisie Alba.

EARNING POTENTIAL: More than $500 per month per kid, depending on how many days you babysit, how many kids you watch, and where you live.

SEASONAL: No, although sometimes your days/hours might get cut. For example, during the summer when children are out of school, clients might hire a niece or nephew to watch their kids.

LICENSE REQUIRED: Maybe, depending on how many kids you watch and your local regulations.

LEGAL CONSIDERATIONS: Incorporate. You don't want to be in a situation where you could be blamed for any kind of abuse. Make sure you have the right business entity in place, and the right insurance policy, as well as a legal agreement with the client. You are caring for a human life!

SAFETY CONSIDERATIONS: You might have to childproof your house, which means different things for different ages. Make sure you understand allergy needs and other special circumstances concerning the child in your care. Also, make sure your pets don't create a safety issue.

LOCAL REGULATIONS: Check to see if there are any government requirements in addition to a business license.

STARTUP COSTS: Possibly nothing. You might find yourself spending a little more at the grocery store. It's not a big deal, but make sure you factor this into what you charge or your margins could disappear. If you are providing regular meals, increase your rate appropriately.

STARTUP NEEDS: You should have a nice, stable environment to welcome the child.

SKILLS NEEDED: Obviously, you should like kids. If you don't like kids, or are impatient with them, pass on this Alternative. First-aid training should be obtained and kept current.

MARKETING / SALES NEEDS: Let your family and friends know you want to babysit, and be sure they know your rate. You don't want to babysit for free just because you are available. Once people find out you are at home and available, people might call to see if you will watch their kid for free for the afternoon. That's not what you are looking for. My wife got all of her babysitting jobs because people knew she was available, they knew she wanted to do it, and that she had good references.

Bookkeeper

According to Robert Kiyosaki, author of The Millionaire Next Door, you should enlist experts when you start your business to help you do the right things the right way. For example, you should have an attorney help you set the business up. Kiyosaki suggests you hire an accountant. I realized I needed someone to help me with my business bookkeeping. By definition, bookkeeping is "the activity or occupation of keeping the financial records of a business."

Bookkeeping doesn't have to include any services other than keeping financial records. As a bookkeeper, you can provide the accountant with the relevant information needed to prepare taxes. If you don't like preparing taxes, tax deadlines are not as busy for you as they are for those who do.

Cheryl Conklin has maintained a successful bookkeeping business for years. She cautions against preparing taxes unless you are registered with the Internal Revenue Service (IRS). She says, "The IRS requires paid tax preparers to be certified. E-filing is strongly encouraged, and you have to jump through hoops to be able to e-file tax returns as a paid preparer."

Cheryl describes her various roles as a bookkeeper, "I had clients where I completed every aspect of their bookkeeping up to tax preparation, and other clients who just wanted me to reconcile bank accounts and calculate payroll taxes. Some clients paid only thirty dollars each month while others paid around $600 per month. Your pay depends on the type and amount of work."

She continues, “If a bookkeeper is handling payroll taxes, January is an extremely busy month reconciling payroll reports and taxes to complete W2s. I’ve made one third of my annual income in January. I also worked sixty hours a week. It gets complicated when the client handles the payroll reporting requirements all year and then asks me to complete the W2s. Mistakes can come back to haunt a bookkeeper because those mistakes could be misconstrued as fraud.”

Bookkeepers are typically trained and sometimes certified, although certification is not a requirement. Many who have performed bookkeeping services without training or certifications have found they like this type of work. Bookkeeping is something that can be done anytime, even at night after the kids are asleep.

Typically, your clients will stay with you for a long time and you don’t have to resell them on your services. You are like a silent partner helping them do something that has to be done, but you aren’t required to be in their offices much, if at all. You can have considerable flexibility in your schedule and travel.

To build your client list, Cheryl suggests, “Start by contacting accounting firms. It’s always nice to have them on your side. They usually have clients they don't want to mess with on a regular basis, but want the big money at the end of the year on the tax return.”

She continues, “Another great way to begin a bookkeeping business is to contact small businesses with whom you already have a relationship. Many times, they are floundering. Accounting firms are pretty pricey and a bookkeeper can provide quality work at a lower cost while allowing the small business to maintain ties with an accounting firm for tax reasons.”

Here are some lessons Cheryl has learned in her business:

- Avoid clients who try to ignore the law. As a bookkeeper, you are on the line for honest reporting. Don't let a client make you push that line.
- The biggest mistake she made was to continue working for a client with financial problems. Even though they kept promising

they were expecting more capital from their investor, she never got paid for that job.
- Another client consistently made mistakes in the books that took a lot of time to find and correct. They always complained about her bill. They didn't always have the money to pay her, their payroll, or their payroll taxes. Because they consistently ignored her recommendations, she finally "fired" them.

What about deadlines and scheduling? Cheryl says, “Payroll reports and taxes must be completed in a timely manner. For a few years, it seemed that every time a family member came to town or invited us out of town, it was around a deadline. The most common deadlines are the tenth, the fifteenth and the last day of the month.”

Cheryl talks about a critical aspect to her business, “Customer service is even more important than bookkeeping knowledge. You can always get more education. I drop everything to help a client meet a deadline because it garners loyalty and it shows my client that their problems are important to me. Sometimes I have to rearrange my personal life to help a client, but it's usually worth it in the long run.”

INSPIRED BY: Cheryl Conklin

EARNING POTENTIAL: One hundred to $1,000 per month per client.

SEASONAL: No.

LICENSE REQUIRED: No.

LEGAL CONSIDERATIONS: Incorporate. Mistakes could result in legal action against you and your client, and problems with the IRS. However, Cheryl warns, “Incorporating won't protect a bookkeeper engaging in fraudulent practices. Even a contract bookkeeper can be held legally responsible for mistakes. Also, limited liability corporation members can have their assets attached in negligence cases.”

SAFETY CONSIDERATIONS: None.

LOCAL REGULATIONS: None.

STARTUP COSTS: Zero to $300.

STARTUP NEEDS: A bookkeeper should have a reliable computer with the right bookkeeping software. If you don't have the right software, your client might buy it for you, or you can pass the cost on to your client.

SKILLS NEEDED: Bookkeepers typically have high attention to detail. You can usually get specialized training from your local community college, or from an online service like UniversalAccounting.com. Training and certifications can help you do your job better, make you more marketable, and increase your confidence in your skills. Confidentiality is a must. Cheryl adds, "In conjunction with the IRS and local accountants, the New Mexico Taxation and Revenue Department puts on monthly seminars regarding proper bookkeeping procedures required by state law as well as how to legally begin a business in the state. Make sure you are following all local laws and licensing guidelines."

MARKETING / SALES NEEDS: The Universal Accounting website states that over five hundred fifty thousand businesses are started each month. That's a lot of prospects for your bookkeeping service! Even if the companies don't bring in significant revenue, network with people at small companies. Any business that files taxes needs bookkeeping services, whether it's performed in house or outsourced to you. Cheryl adds, "My business was generated strictly from word of mouth. A Certified Public Accountant referred my first clients to me and that client referred the rest. Word of mouth is the best advertising for a bookkeeper because a potential client needs to know you are trustworthy."

Cotton Candy Machine Rental

My cousin, Jordan Willison, has always been an entrepreneur. While in college, he had the sweet idea to buy a commercial cotton candy machine and rent it out for parties. Because he lived in a town with two major universities, his cotton candy machine always seemed to be rented out.

Jordan says, "Owning a cotton candy machine rental business takes up front cash to get started, which can be a potential obstacle. I have owned three machines during my cotton candy career. The first one cost $1,200 and paid for itself within three months. The following two were paid off within one month because I built a solid clientele and knew what I was doing."

Jordan provided customers with the machine and everything needed to make cotton candy. He rented it out to church clubs, school groups, family reunions, and any type of get together that wanted to add a fun element to their event. Cotton candy is always a fun addition to a party, right?

Jordan started small with only one machine. He relates, "I advertised on Craigslist and in the classified section of a local news website. After I built some capital, I paid for advertisements on Facebook. This helped me build a strong client base. I eventually scaled back my Facebook ads and focused on free advertising. I also made business cards and put at least ten cards in the supplies bag with each order. When customers came to pick up the machine, I would mention the cards and ask them to give my cards to anyone who asked about the machine."

As the machine owner, you need to make sure the machine is returned in good order. You will train customers on how to operate and clean the machine, but there could be problems. What if it is returned damaged? What about regular maintenance? Jordan responds, "I found the people renting the machine were generally good people. They were usually doing fundraisers." Because he trusted his clients with his expensive machine, the caliber of his clients was important.

This could be an easy, low-key Alternative that could grow to where other rental types make sense, such as popcorn poppers and snow cone machines. The key to success is keeping your machine(s) rented.

Jordan shares, "I often made more money by selling the supplies than the rental. I made my own floss sugar. NEVER buy premade sugar unless you're in a jam. I stocked up on twenty-five-pound bags of sugar when they went on sale for about ten dollars a bag. Then I mixed in about fifty cents worth of flossine. If you purchased the same amount of floss sugar online, or in a store, it would cost well over a hundred dollars."

For as little as one hour a week cleaning the machine and getting supplies ready for customers, Jordan found he could potentially make $200 to $300 by keeping his machine renting. What could be more fun than that? This is a great business to operate while going to school or working full time. It's also a great way to teach business skills to your children.

Jordan said, "Make sure you always have supplies on hand. 95 percent of your customers will not have floss, sugar, or paper cones just sitting in their garage. If a customer wants to rent your machine but you forgot to order more supplies, chances are they will take their business elsewhere."

He continues, "A good back-up plan is to partner with a local rental company. I made a deal with a local rental store manager. If I had a customer who wanted a machine while mine were booked, I would send them to the rental store. That store would do the same for me. This referral system is a little touch-and-go at first but once you develop a strong relationship with the manager, it can pay off. If you run out of supplies, you can still rent your machine and refer your clients to the rental store for supplies. Make sure your customers tell the store you sent them. By sending clients to the rental store, you are more likely to get reciprocal referrals when the rental store is booked."

INSPIRED BY: Jordan Willison, CottonCandyConcessions.com.

EARNING POTENTIAL: One hundred dollars to $1,000 monthly, depending on how many machines you have and how many nights they are rented.

SEASONAL: Parties are year round, but this can be seasonal. Jordan says, "Business fell significantly in the winter months. It would be at its peak around the summer holidays so I raised my prices. The 4th of July is probably the biggest opportunity. I tripled my prices for the holiday weekend. I have made about $400 from renting one machine during that weekend. It takes a lot of planning and coordination so be sure to stay on top of it."

LICENSE REQUIRED: You don't need a license to rent the machine and sell the supplies. However, a license is required if you make the cotton candy and sell it yourself. When he first started his business, Jordan made the cotton candy to sell, but found it was too time-consuming and much easier to rent the machine out. Check your local regulations to see if this is true where you do business.

LEGAL CONSIDERATIONS: Incorporate.

SAFETY CONSIDERATIONS: Make sure the unit is clean before you rent it. Properly explain the machine operation to every customer. Point out the factory safety stickers on the machine.

LOCAL REGULATIONS: Check with your city.

STARTUP COSTS: At least $200 for a used machine on eBay or more than $500 for new machines. Budget an additional one hundred dollars for supplies to sell to your clients. Jordan shares advice on buying the right machine, "My machines cost about $900 each. Add another $150 for the plastic bubble and one hundred dollars for initial supplies. I went with a well-known name brand and bought the easiest machine with only one button for customers to use. Heat and power have to be adjusted on other models, making it easier for customers to break."

STARTUP NEEDS: The cotton candy machine, accessories, and supplies.

SKILLS NEEDED: You should be able to manage clients, deliver and receive equipment, and prepare for the next client. Training clients to operate and clean the machine properly is essential.

MARKETING / SALES NEEDS: Anyone who is putting on an event with lots of people, especially children, could be your client. You might have a corporate client one weekend, a family reunion the next weekend, and a church gathering the following weekend. Word of mouth should be a powerful part of your strategy, but you also will need to reach out to clubs and groups to let them know what you have available. You could do this with special business/marketing cards, or through social marketing channels. Jordan adds, "You can get a permit from the county to set up a folding advertising board on corners near elementary schools." People putting on events might not think about renting a cotton candy machine, or they might assume it is too expensive or hard to operate. Show them how easy and affordable it is to have one at their party!

Heavy Equipment Rental & Leasing

I was talking to a friend about this book and he said, "You have to include my buddy's company! He bought a crane, leased it, and now has a bunch of cranes and large machinery. He makes a fortune!" My friend was talking about Mountain Crane, which supposedly grosses millions of dollars each year and is the largest crane rental company in this area.

I didn't initially want to include this idea as an Alternative because it could take a lot of money to get started. I don't expect you to acquire the tens or hundreds of thousands of dollars to buy your first tower crane for leasing. You would also need a place to store the crane or other equipment when it is not rented. You would need special insurance and legal coverage, as well as specialized sales talent to find customers. It might be too far out of your comfort zone.

Even if you haven't thought about a business like this, you might have what it takes to make it work. A quick online search shows you can rent a tower crane for $1,000 to $3,000 per hour, and sometimes up to $30,000 each month. Successfully renting out tower cranes will take a lot of work but the money and the demand are there. As long as commercial building is healthy, there will be a need for machinery and tools. You don't want to compete with Home Depot and local small machinery rental companies. This niche is for specific customers with specific projects.

This business is simply about supply and demand. Construction will happen. In a boom time, it can be hard to obtain the right equipment for finishing buildings on time. Even if your expertise is outside the construction world, you might have what it takes to start a business like this. If you can get the equipment to lease but don't know the industry, perhaps you could partner with someone who does. The cost for one crane is less than the cost to start many franchises, and you can operate the business by your own rules and policies. If you are in the right location at the right time, you might take advantage of a building boom, which could be very profitable.

As an exercise, take twenty minutes to sketch out a business plan as if you were going to move forward on a business like this. Can you figure out solutions to the challenges listed above? If you can, maybe you can create a fun, sustainable business you can run from a comfortable home office. Just because you rent tower cranes doesn't mean you operate them. You might be busy enough managing the sales and paperwork part of the job.

If tower cranes aren't for you, what could you rent or lease to others? There are always things in demand that people or companies don't want to own, store or maintain. This could be your opportunity to provide a solution for them and create an income for you.

INSPIRED BY: Mountain Crane, MountainCrane.com.

EARNING POTENTIAL: Tens of thousands per month and more, depending on your inventory and the market.

SEASONAL: Depends on what you rent.

LICENSE REQUIRED: Check with your city.

LEGAL CONSIDERATIONS: Incorporate. Have attorneys draw up the appropriate contracts and agreements to decrease your liability.

SAFETY CONSIDERATIONS: There are a lot of potential safety hazards. Become a safety expert and ensure your clients are trained with signed paperwork to cover liability for operator error. Consult with insurance and attorneys who specialize in this.

LOCAL REGULATIONS: Check with your city.

STARTUP COSTS: Depends on what you want to lease. Consult MachineryTrader.com for price ranges.

STARTUP NEEDS: You need a place to store your machinery and transportation to the client's site. You should be ready to provide a team for transporting the equipment, setting it up and taking it down, and possibly even operate it.

SKILLS NEEDED: You need to understand the leasing and commercial construction industries. You might focus on one area, like sales, but you'll need others who can specialize in setup and operation. Acquiring a customer and delivering your products and services is very involved.

MARKETING / SALES NEEDS: Your market will be qualified customers who have very specific needs. Where do you find these customers? How do you let them know about your needs? Network with construction companies, construction project managers, crane operators, commercial lenders, commercial realtors, and anyone involved in the commercial building space. Make your services known and make it easy for people to talk about you.

Curb Number Painter

A friend told me about a quick and easy way he made money as a teenager. Because he didn't have financial obligations, his goal was to make just forty dollars each time he went out. He said he could do this within one hour by painting house numbers on the curb in front of houses.

Partnering with a friend, they would take turns knocking on doors and painting house numbers on the curb. Their equipment consisted of number templates and spray paint. Between talking to the homeowner and painting the curbs, they made more per hour than some people with a "real job" make!

I haven't seen any organized competition in this space, so with less than hundred dollars of supplies, you can make money while you make the neighborhood safer. The pitch is simple: If an emergency vehicle is looking for the house number, a freshly painted number on the curb is easier to find.

An enterprising person could do this in the evenings and on the weekends, potentially bringing in enough to pay some bills and maybe even make the house payment. I found a story of a college student who claimed to make $80,000 a year painting numbers on curbs. I think this is a very high expectation, but the work and the money are there. I tried this Alternative while writing this book and found that I could regularly make forty dollars an hour.

This is a mobile business. My equipment fits in my trunk and I travel from neighborhood to neighborhood. The biggest challenge is travelling to other cities where a different permit may be required. I have a solicitor's permit for my own city but not any surrounding cities.

This business is fun, and you can do it with other people. You can have fancy design options including different templates, number styles and paint colors. Or, you can simplify by offering black numbers on a white background with one number style. Simple means fast and easy, and only one decision to make for the customer. Fancier means you can upsell based on colors or designs.

Since I started painting numbers on curbs, I can't drive through a neighborhood and see a faded number without associating a twenty dollar sale to that house!

INSPIRED BY: Brady Dow, my neighbor who did this as a teenager.

EARNING POTENTIAL: Forty dollars per hour, depending on what you charge.

SEASONAL: This is not much fun in cold weather and impossible to do in the rain.

LICENSE REQUIRED: You will usually need a license or permit to knock on doors.

LEGAL CONSIDERATIONS: None.

SAFETY CONSIDERATIONS: This is a pretty simple business. I think the only danger I faced was going door to door, and then painting the numbers while sitting in the curb.

LOCAL REGULATIONS: Check with your city to find out if a solicitation license or other permission is required.

STARTUP COSTS: Less than one hundred dollars.

STARTUP NEEDS: Number templates and at least two colors of spray paint (background color and number color). You might be able to start this business for less than twenty-five dollars. I bought disposable craft paintbrushes for touching up the painted numbers.

SKILLS NEEDED: A thick skin and an easygoing manner are essential for door-to-door sales. Working with spray paint can be frustrating, but you'll develop your system with masking tape and other tools to help you paint a sharp background and numbers for the client.

MARKETING / SALES NEEDS: Ask for referrals. You can go door to door, use social media, and distribute flyers to get pre-orders. Our greatest success came from going door to door, but someone in my neighborhood simply leaves signup flyers on my doorknob.

Daycare Provider

In another Alternative, I explored babysitting as a way to make money. There are usually state regulations about how many children you can have in your home per adult. (Search “staff/child ratio” for more information.) For example, a babysitter can’t watch twenty kids. That is what I would call a daycare. Daycares operate under different requirements and regulations.

My aunt, Diana Marley, ran a successful daycare business in Long Beach, California, for decades. Over the years she has seen many things, many of them heartwarming, some of them heartbreaking. She developed special bonds with both the children and their parents. Many have since grown, married, and had their own kids! Diana has been invited to the weddings of some of the children who were in her daycare.

Diana’s business thrived to a point where she had employees and a recurring monthly income. The daycare business model is great for developing repeat income, since most clients pay weekly or monthly as long as they perceive things are going well. Many daycares have waiting lists, meaning they’ve gotten to the point where they don’t need to market. Their prospects are lined up, waiting for a chance to become a client!

Diana shares how she kept her daycare full, “Network with other providers to exchange ideas, rates, and tips on hiring help. I charged less than most of the providers around me and I always gave discounts if more than one child in a family was enrolling. I did not charge an enrollment fee. I did not get special insurance. Instead, I asked parents to sign a waiver of liability. I didn't have to do very much advertising other than using parent referrals."

Diana talks about how to earn a higher margin in your daycare business, "Don't try to do it all by yourself. A twelve-child daycare isn't much more work, and the money is twice as good. Get a license for twelve even if you don't use it. It requires a little more effort to obtain but you can start alone and hire an assistant when you need one."

She continues, "You will make good money if you are organized and present a clean, safe atmosphere. If you are a good provider, you will prosper through word-of-mouth advertising, which is the best kind. In California, I made between $5,000 and $6,000 per month."

A daycare can take a lot of work to set up, including modifying your home and obtaining proper equipment. Once you have clients, your schedule revolves around the daycare. You start early in the morning and end late in the evening. Planning vacations and holidays can be tricky. You can't take a day off if you are tired or not in the mood.

This business is not for the faint of heart, but it can be rewarding, financially and in other ways.

INSPIRED BY: Diana Marley, retired daycare owner.

EARNING POTENTIAL: Hundreds per month per kid.

SEASONAL: No, although business might decline in the summer months.

LICENSE REQUIRED: Yes.

LEGAL CONSIDERATIONS: There are many legal considerations. Make sure you follow all appropriate regulations, get certified and licensed, and have appropriate measures in place to avoid accusations and prevent emergencies.

SAFETY CONSIDERATIONS: There are many safety considerations. The lives and well being of little ones are in your hands. To get licensed as a daycare service provider, you will have many safety checks that should help you prepare a safe environment.

LOCAL REGULATIONS: This is a highly regulated business.

STARTUP COSTS: Zero to thousands of dollars to modify your home to meet regulations.

STARTUP NEEDS: You need to have a place for the daycare, usually a room at your house. I've seen garages converted into the daycare area, with separate entrances to the yard. Yards need to be enclosed and safe. It's fun to walk into someone's daycare and see all the stuff that helps it run smoothly, from books and toys, to low tables for art projects, and places to put jackets and shoes.

SKILLS NEEDED: You should be patient and loving with children, as well as flexible and resourceful, since you never know what each day will bring. This is a high-demand business and you can't call in sick if you are tired.

MARKETING / SALES NEEDS: Good daycare providers are always in demand. If you provide the right environment and delight your clients, they'll tell their neighbors about you. If you are in a high-traffic area, signage at your house might be all you need. You can advertise with flyers and ads online, or just keep it word of mouth through your trusted friends, neighbors and network. Parents are continually looking for backup daycare solutions. Visit other daycares in your area to establish relationships with those providers. They might refer parents to you if they are full.

Dog Walker

The pet industry is massive. In a quick search online, I learned 62 percent of American households, or over 73 million homes, own a pet. In 2011, pet owners spent over $50 billion on food, products and services. You probably know lots of dog owners, many of whom don't have a lot of time to give all the attention their beloved pet needs. Have you thought about selling your time to help them? Dog owners know their dogs need to be walked regularly, even if they have access to a big yard.

There are many websites claiming dogs need to be walked every day. When I owned dogs, I felt guilty when they didn't get their daily walk. How do you take care of that, though, when you are busy? Easy! You hire someone to walk your dog! Siobhan Oldham is a professional dog walker in the Los Angeles area who shared details and insights about this Alternative.

Siobhan takes clients' dogs on hikes in the Hollywood hills and surrounding areas. She is passionate about giving them a hearty workout. She offers various related services, including trips to the beach, daycare, boarding, and even in-home pet sitting. She also has a passion for leatherwork, which she channels into a revenue stream by making collars and related products.

If you have time, good health, and a love for dogs, this could be a great Alternative for you. Since people are at school or work, there are a lot of empty homes in my neighborhood during the day. That results in a lot of bored and under-exercised dogs. I'm sure someone in my neighborhood could offer services to the many dog owners who want a better life for their dogs.

Siobhan shares some of the reasons her clients hire her. If you choose to offer these services, consider using this information as you communicate your value proposition to prospects. She says, “A third of my clients want their dogs exercised to release excess energy which helps curb destructive behavior. Another third want their dogs to be part of a pack and have a social life. The last third are apartment dwellers who just need help letting their dog out so it can go to the bathroom in the middle of the day.”

Siobhan shares some of the perks of this business, “You actually get paid to exercise. Plus you get paid to receive animal therapy. The dogs give you affection and unconditional love. Give them a good walk, some affection, and they are eternally grateful. Your income is spread out over multiple clients so client turnover doesn’t have much of an impact. You have great flexibility with your schedule.”

How do you get clients? Siohban shares, “My best marketing strategy was branding my vehicle. I had a professional partial wrap of my logo blown up so the dog is jumping along the back of my truck. It’s fun and eye catching, and instantly conveys my business. People contact me because they saw my vehicle and looked up my website. Getting decals legitimized my business and built brand recognition.”

She continues, “Be reliable! Showing up on time, every time, is very important. Take time to share moments of the dog’s day with your clients. When a client is out of town, I take a photo on my phone and text it to them with a cute message from their pets. Understand how much communication each client needs to feel satisfied and confident that their pets are receiving attention and care. One person may appreciate a text or photo once a month while another may need a text every day.”

Do you need to have a big yard for this Alternative be an option? Siohban says, “People think they need a house with a yard to offer this service. It’s simply not true. I have a studio apartment with no yard. People know I will take their dog on a hike, or to the mountains.”

To be successful, Siobhan suggests, "Own a dog so you understand people's concerns and can have empathy. People will ask you lots of questions about the dogs including diet, bad habits, or medical conditions. No one expects you to have all the answers, but you need to be emotionally invested in your clients' pets and help them find solutions." She adds, "Take a dog handling class from a professional trainer. Not from a box chain pet store, but an actual dog handling class."

INSPIRED BY: Siobhan Oldham, ballandbone.com.

EARNING POTENTIAL: Siohban says, "Up to $6,000 a month with an established clientele."

SEASONAL: Bad weather can make it uncomfortable but dogs need to walk every day.

LICENSE REQUIRED: Though you don't need a license for walking the dogs, make sure the dogs you walk are licensed.

LEGAL CONSIDERATIONS: Siobhan recommends you get liability insurance.

SAFETY CONSIDERATIONS: This is a strenuous job. Siobhan says, "Do not take dogs with aggressive tendencies because the liability risk is too huge."

LOCAL REGULATIONS: Siobhan says, "There are restrictions as to how many dogs you can walk at once in public parks."

STARTUP COSTS: None.

STARTUP NEEDS: You need time, good walking shoes, and customers. Transportation to pick up the dogs is helpful.

SKILLS NEEDED: You must like dogs and be able to endure the hikes with them. Siobhan adds, "The ability to sell your services is critical."

MARKETING / SALES NEEDS: Focus on word of mouth through the dog-owning community. You can offer your services online, like Siobhan does, but you don't need to have a web presence to be successful. Get business cards or something like a branded bag with doggie treats customers can pass along to their friends. You need to instill trust amongst your customers and prospects since you'll be with one of their most valued family members. Siobhan says, "When I was starting out, I shot a video of the trail I was walking with the dogs and I had a photographer take photos of me interacting with my clients' dogs." She continues, "Business cards are critical. Putting the vinyl decals on my vehicle has paid for itself many times over, allowing clients to contact me directly as well as build brand recognition."

Doorknob Flyer Distributor

When I was a teenager, a neighbor invited me and my friends to help him with his business. He paid us minimum wage to distribute flyers throughout neighborhoods by hanging them on door knobs. It was grunt work and I didn't love it. But I was intrigued by my neighbor and his business, especially since I had not grown up around many entrepreneurs.

To make money doing this, you need to find a business that wants to get in front of a local audience. Your clientele might include a restaurant, a realtor, a garage door business or any number of local businesses you might not even know. There are more businesses around you than you might guess. A directory of businesses registered in my relatively small town of 20,000 people indicates there are somewhere near 1,000 incorporated businesses. That's a lot of small businesses!

An online search shows there are small companies, usually with one or two people, who offer this service. From an online forum, I learned this is an easy business to get into, and that you can get regular work from your clients. Someone on the forum wrote, "I am the owner of a very small computer repair business in The Woodlands. I desperately need somebody to deliver door hangers for me. Not sure if you would service The Woodlands, but please contact me if you do or if you know somebody that does."*

Even though today's marketing strategies seem to focus on online marketing, this type of work is still in demand. From that same forum, I read posts by people who do this work for a living and with systems and teams in place. It looks like you can make this business as big as you want.

Someone on the forum commented that you have to be careful of local regulations as there are fines if you don't abide by the local laws. There are discussions about how it is easier to do this in some cities, while other cities have stricter ordinances. For example, someone in Houston said it's easier to do than in Seattle. A Seattleite responded that it is possible to do just fine there. Aside from laws, different areas would have different challenges such as labor costs, weather, terrain (hills versus flat streets), proximity of houses to one another, and other elements.

As with any business, price yourself appropriately so you make a good margin. You might be tempted to lower your prices just to get a job, but it might not be profitable. Understand your costs (including flyer design and printing) to know how much you can charge and still maintain a healthy profit margin.

INSPIRED BY: One of my earliest bosses but I don't remember his name.

EARNING POTENTIAL: Hundreds of dollars per client.

SEASONAL: Perhaps.

LICENSE REQUIRED: Possibly. Check local laws. Violations are usually costly.

LEGAL CONSIDERATIONS: Incorporate.

SAFETY CONSIDERATIONS: You and/or your employees or subcontractors will walk onto private property. Be careful of safety hazards and be respectful to people's property.

LOCAL REGULATIONS: Check with your city.

STARTUP COSTS: Less than one hundred dollars.

STARTUP NEEDS: Once you have a client, flyers, and rubber bands or something to hang the flyer with, you won't need more than good walking shoes.

SKILLS NEEDED: You need to sell the service to the client as well as coordinate flyer production and delivery. You should have (or will develop) project management, sales, management, and organizational skills. For instance, your clients might ask you for advice on the flyer's design (a service you could upsell).

MARKETING / SALES NEEDS: Network with local businesses that are open to trying a targeted local blitz. Chamber of Commerce meetings might be great places to meet clients. Don't be afraid to go into stores and talk to the manager. Check your city offices to see if they have a list of local businesses that are registered in the city limits.

*http://smallbusinessonlinecommunity.bankofamerica.com/message/87758

Event Planner

As a professional speaker, I've been to many events around the country. Some events were well organized while others had multiple flaws. There are indicators as to how successful an event might be, or how nourished and inspired attendees will be when they leave. Audience size is one of those signs. If someone says to expect one hundred people, and there are only twenty-five, I know I'm not spending my time or money well at that event.

So many elements go into planning and executing a successful event. As a business owner, I want to get as many "butts in seats," as they say in the speaking industry, as possible. It helps my business grow and can lead to more sales. Organizations want to get a lot of people at their events because they can easily measure their return on the investment in the event by the number of attendees. They plan for future events based on the successes (or failures) of past events.

A good event planner is critical in driving the event's success. Event planning can be done by different people. Associations and universities might have an event planner on staff. Volunteer organizations usually have a volunteer who spearheads the events committee, finds speakers, and makes sure the venue is ready. Sometimes the person planning an event has experience with event planning, sometimes they are thrown into it with no experience.

Michelle Thompson, a Certified Meeting Professional (CMP), shares, "Nonprofit organizations often execute their events with volunteer committees. A staff member may become the committee chairperson and the remaining roles are filled with volunteers who are in charge of one aspect of the event. There might be a marketing volunteer, a catering volunteer, or an entertainment volunteer. This spreads out the burden of the work, but that has its own challenges during the planning process."

If I can work with an experienced event planner, I feel better about the event. I know it will be advertised well, the room will be ready, I'll have my needs met, and the event details will not be ignored. If I'm speaking at an event without an experienced planner, I know I'll have to spend more time helping set up and addressing issues that might arise.

If you're a professional event planner, you know how BIG this job can be. You also know how stressful it can be dealing with all the parties involved. If you aren't a professional event planner, but have what it takes to make an event successful, I might hire you to make my events more successful. You'll need to be organized, ambitious, and creative. Challenges include finding the right venue, making sure the marketing is done before and after the event, filling the venue, as well as working with multiple parties to make the event successful.

If you are serious about pursuing a career as an event planner, consider joining Meeting Professionals International (mpiweb.org), the organization for event professionals. I've worked with many people who have enough skills or experience to make an event successful. Are you one of them?

INSPIRED BY: Michelle Thompson, CMP, peacockevents.com, and many of the professional and volunteer meeting planners who have helped coordinate my speaking engagements. Michelle wrote a workbook about planning events with committees. Here's the link: peacockevents.com/design-by-committee-workbook.

EARNING POTENTIAL: $500 or more per meeting.

SEASONAL: No, although summers can be quiet for speakers. Consider camps and family reunions and other events as non-speaker events you could organize.

LICENSE REQUIRED: No.

LEGAL CONSIDERATIONS: Incorporate. Michelle says, "There are no legal requirements, but I highly recommend a general liability policy for anyone planning events or meetings."

SAFETY CONSIDERATIONS: Michelle says, "I have often found myself lifting and carrying heavy boxes, signage, and packages." Having been involved in many events, I'd add there might be mental considerations approaching insanity as you get closer to the event.

LOCAL REGULATIONS: None.

STARTUP COSTS: Zero.

STARTUP NEEDS: A phone and computer system since you'll be communicating and organizing a lot. You should use a customer relationship management system, like JibberJobber.com, to keep track of tasks and contacts.

SKILLS NEEDED: You need to have strong organizational skills and a passion for detail, as well as the ability to handle changes in a high-stress environment. You might market and sell to all kinds of people, including selling a potential audience on attending, pitching an opportunity to a speaker, selling sponsorships to businesses, and selling last-minute changes to the caterer or venue host. Michelle says these three skills are essential: goal setting, budget management, and contract negotiation skills.

MARKETING / SALES NEEDS: Your clients typically will be businesses unless you focus on a specific consumer market, like organizing family reunions. Network online and face to face. Find other professional speakers by researching the local National Speakers Association chapter. Be where they are, gain their trust, and help them understand your value and what they miss if they don't hire you. Your audience can include solopreneurs, realtors, speakers, companies, and more.

Homebound Hair Care

My wife, Kaisie, earned her cosmetology certificate early in our marriage, and started working in a salon. There were some things she liked about the salon and some things she disliked. Eventually, it became clear that she should move out of that salon. But she was determined to replace that income. She came up with a great idea: She could make money going to the houses of people who could not physically go to a salon.

By starting her own business, Kaisie freed up her schedule and chose her clients. As an employee of the salon, she was required to be there certain days at certain times, and she sometimes found herself working with people she did not choose. When she started her homebound hair care business, she was able to decide what hours she wanted to work, and build her own client list. Of course, this Alternative requires a cosmetology license, but I'm including it in this book because I want to show an option to what most cosmetologists do when they finish school.

We have fond memories of visiting a particular client my wife serviced. The client's husband, Hyrum, was always in the mood to chat and tell stories. Hyrum's wife had suffered a stroke and couldn't talk or communicate well. Watching Hyrum interact with his wife and helping Kaisie understand how his wife wanted her hair done was very tender. While enjoying interacting with Hyrum, Kaisie massaged his wife's scalp, and washed and styled her hair.

It was very fulfilling work for Kaisie because she could do two things she loved to do: serve others through helping them feel clean and beautiful, and interact with people. I think Hyrum enjoyed the visits as much as his wife did. Hyrum longed for interaction with others and was lonely since he couldn't communicate well with his wife. I know he appreciated someone who treated his wife with gentle love.

My wife made more per hour than at a salon. People expected to pay more since the services required travel and setup time, and were harder to provide in someone's home. Because this business didn't have much competition, Kaisie was able to set her own prices. She could do what she wanted, like giving long scalp massages, without worrying about a boss who watched the clock and made her produce more. My wife was not bound to the politics of a salon. Many cosmetologists think their options are limited to working at a salon as an employee, leasing a chair at a salon as a contractor, or opening a salon at their own house. Even though she didn't pursue any of those options, my wife was able to work in her field and provide personalized service.

Homebound hair care gets around the cost and hassle of putting in a salon. This business is a great example of starting something that can lead to additional revenue streams.

In most places, you cannot run a salon out of your house unless you meet certain requirements. You need to be a licensed cosmetologist and you must have a home salon approved by the state. This usually means you have to have a separate entrance and a sink. You can easily spend $10,000 just to make a room or garage ready to pass the state inspection for qualifying as a home salon. If you rent, or are in a condominium, this is not an option. Homebound hair care gets around the cost and hassle of putting in a salon.

This business is a great example of starting something that can lead to additional revenue streams. If you look up homebound services online, you'll see companies that offer additional services, such as personal care, companionship, transportation, meal preparation, light housekeeping, and other choices. If you gain the trust of your client, they might give you additional and related business.

INSPIRED BY: My wife, Kaisie Alba.

EARNING POTENTIAL: Depends on your location. Probably from thirty to fifty dollars per visit.

SEASONAL: No.

LICENSE REQUIRED: You must be a licensed cosmetologist.

LEGAL CONSIDERATIONS: Incorporate. Normally, it is against the law to provide cosmetology service outside of a salon or home salon. In many places, if the person cannot go to a salon, you can do it at their location. Check state and local regulations. Also, talk to an insurance specialist to ensure you have the proper insurance in place to do this type of work.

SAFETY CONSIDERATIONS: Because there are chemical and cleanliness issues, the safety practices will be similar to those in a salon. Since you are working in different environments, you might find new safety hazards, like bending over a kitchen sink in an awkward way while you rinse the client's hair.

LOCAL REGULATIONS: Check with your state licensing organization to ensure you are compliant with regulations and laws.

STARTUP COSTS: None, assuming you still have your tools from cosmetology school.

STARTUP NEEDS: Transportation to your client's location and the equipment you used while obtaining your cosmetology certificate. If you don't have a license, do not attempt this Alternative because penalties can be significant.

SKILLS NEEDED: In addition to what you learned at school, you need to be strong enough to help people who might have limited physical ability to get to the sink. As I remember, this was tricky for Kaisie.

MARKETING / SALES NEEDS: Word-of-mouth referrals should help you grow a strong business. Get referrals from nursing homes and businesses who know about homebound patients. Caretakers usually network with other caretakers and would be happy to tell others about your services if you are reasonably priced, and respect and delight their loved ones.

Home Stager

I connected with Karen Otto shortly after she started her "home staging" business. I had never heard of home staging and asked her to explain it to me. What I learned was intriguing and exciting.

Home staging is what you do to a house to prepare it for sale. When a prospective buyer walks in, you want them to think, "Wow, this is the home I've always wanted!" Staging, decorating, and preparing the home can significantly impact the length of time it takes to sell the home as well as the purchase price. Imagine walking into a home that looks like someone else's everyday lived-in house with regular decorations compared to walking into a home that has been staged and looks picture perfect!

To some extent, Realtors take on this task, but they can bring in a professional home stager like Karen. Some people find it easy and fun to decorate their living space, but many people (like me) find it tedious and confusing, especially with all of the other house-selling details that need to be handled. Hiring a home stager can free you up to focus on other things.

Karen says, "While it doesn't take a lot of financial capital, you do need to have creative capital." I know I don't have the necessary creative capital, but I bet some of you have an abundance of it!

She continues, "Treat this as you would any small business and consider taking a business class or home staging training with a company that can help you understand the business model and intricacies of a home staging business. While knowing how to stage is one thing, being in business is quite another. Even if you are doing this as a part-time, side income, it's best to understand the basic staging business model."

She explains that there are misconceptions as to what staging is. Many in the real estate industry are under the mistaken belief that staging is expensive and only for high-end homes. Any seller with a house at any price point can use home staging to market and prepare their property for sale. A home staging consultation gives the seller a big bang for their buck and the information they need to do the work themselves.

INSPIRED BY: Karen Otto, HomeStarStaging.com.

EARNING POTENTIAL: Rates vary by location. You should be able to charge at least seventy-five dollars per hour.

SEASONAL: No, but more houses may be on the market during some seasons than others.

LICENSE REQUIRED: No. Look into the certifications available to home stagers.

LEGAL CONSIDERATIONS: Karen says, "Sole proprietorship and LLCs are common amongst home stagers. Having an agreement or contract is something no stager should work without. It protects both the stager and the client and lays out the conditions of the services provided. And it establishes what will, or won't, be okay with each party. For example, I take before-and-after photos to use for marketing. The clients aren't identified by name in the marketing materials. However, I've had some who do NOT want the 'before' photos of their homes online. This is clarified in the contract."

SAFETY CONSIDERATIONS: "Get liability insurance and coverage for inventory you assemble and keep," advises Karen. "If you break a client's priceless antique or scratch a newly finished wood floor, you want to make sure you are covered."

LOCAL REGULATIONS: Because every area is different, Karen recommends registering the business with your local county or city office. Consult an accountant to check whether you have to collect local or state taxes on sales, inventory rentals or your services.

STARTUP COSTS: You can start the business without capital. However, Karen says your initial investment may be as much as $5,000. Below are some possible startup expenses:

- Local business registration.
- Enrollment in a home staging training course such as the one Karen teaches. Most courses include simple contracts that can save you lots of money.
- The appropriate business insurance.
- Website setup and design.
- Business cards.
- A tool kit for hanging artwork, removing nails, and other minor tasks.
- A digital camera for taking before-and-after photos.
- General office supplies including paper, folders, computer, and/or fax machine.
- A merchant account for accepting credit cards. Consider setting up a free Paypal business account.
- A storage facility for keeping inventory.
- Inventory, if you'll be renting furniture and accessories to clients.
- Association dues for RESA (realestatestagingassociation.com), local Realtor boards, and other networking groups.

STARTUP NEEDS: Though many home stagers only offer in-house consultations, Karen also offers telephone consulting or "e-staging." If you meet with clients at the home, you should have good transportation and a professional appearance. How you appear to your prospective clients will significantly impact your ability to get the job, and referrals, since this service is all about image.

SKILLS NEEDED: Aside from the obvious – attention to detail – a vision for design is essential. Other helpful skills include organization, ability to work with existing resources as well as conceptualizing the impact of furniture, home decor, accessories, and paint. The ability to work under pressure and tight timeframes is especially crucial.

MARKETING / SALES NEEDS: Karen says that a strong Internet presence is key because most people start their search for services and products online. Clients are real estate agents and home sellers. Network with real estate agents and brokers, and maintain strong relationships with them. Be able to quantify the return on investment, or value, of your services. The value isn't that you make the house prettier, but that your service helps sell it faster and for more money. That message has to be abundantly clear.

HOME/OFFICE ORGANIZER

I confess I'm something of a slob. Combine a bit of procrastination with various attention-to-detail deficiencies, and a high priority of doing things for my business rather than preparing my environment and the result is a workspace that, well, is not pretty. Somehow, I can focus my attention on my monitor and get my job done even though my office is a mess.

I heard a professional speaker once say, "Design the system, and then HONOR the system." Her message was that we need to create an organizational system and then actually use it, instead of continually tweaking or ignoring it and reverting to old habits.

I don't have the training, experience or interest to make the time to design my organizational system. So I just ignore the clutter and focus on my work.

Yes, I feel guilty just writing this.

Some of you are, as FlyLady (flylady.net) would say, "born organizers." My nine-year-old daughter is a born organizer. She'll ask if she can reorganize the kitchen or bathroom drawers, and she thinks that is thrilling! Where she got that passion is beyond me and her mom! But she's naturally good at it.

If you have a knack for cleaning or organizing, you are blessed with something the rest of us wish we had! And there's money to be made with your talents. What if you don't have a knack for organizing? This can still be a viable Alternative for you. You'll actually be more empathetic if you had to take that journey in becoming organized.

Professional organizer Marla Dee says, "Helping others get organized is NOT the same as doing it for yourself. It's like the difference between being great at a sport versus coaching others to be great. ORGANIZING IS A SKILL. Being able to teach and transfer the skill is critical to your success as a professional organizer. Otherwise, it is simply straightening up stuff, which is something a good house cleaner can do."

She continues, "You must understand that 90 percent of the population is NOT born with the organizing gene. They don't get it. You wouldn't expect a child to read a book if he had never been taught the alphabet. It is the same with organizing. The problem is not that people are lazy, stupid or haven't tried. They just haven't been taught. Don't expect your client to be like you. This is why they NEED YOU. Their struggle needs to be honored and is a gift to you. Otherwise there wouldn't be a need for professional organizers."

If you could fix my organizational problem, I would gladly pay you. You could negotiate a higher fee if I knew you would provide a workable long-term solution that I would use. I'm sure I'm less productive because of my organizational challenges. And my office is off limits to visitors because I don't want them to see that the JibberJobber World Headquarters is a mess.

I'm sharing this with you because you might have a desperately needed skill. Sound interesting? To learn more about professional organizers, review the National Association of Professional Organizers website (NAPO.net). And go to Marla Dee's website, ClearSimple.com, for more resources.

If this sounds like the perfect business for you, you can make additional money running corporate workshops. Hands-on organizing is only one way to monetize this skill.

Marla shares the following tips:

- Get training on how to help others get organized. It is NOT enough to just be good at it for yourself. The training will help you transfer your skills.

- Become a member of NAPO to take advantage of the teleclasses for beginners.
- Get training on how to deliver excellent customer service. This is a highly sensitive service. Professional organizers see things that no one else sees – not the spouse, family, doctor, or friends. Most people hide their clutter and chaos.
- Treat this as a business from the beginning. Marla recommends Service Corps of Retired Executives (score.org), or similar organizations to learn the basics of owning a business.
- Because this is a service business, all your relationships are important. Nurture all connections and research how to create strong alliances.

INSPIRED BY: Marla Dee, ClearSimple.com

EARNING POTENTIAL: Hundreds of dollars per client.

SEASONAL: No.

LICENSE REQUIRED: Marla says a business license is required.

LEGAL CONSIDERATIONS: Incorporate.

SAFETY CONSIDERATIONS: You'll be in a client's home or office where you might encounter a dangerously messy space.

LOCAL REGULATIONS: None.

STARTUP COSTS: Zero to $1,250.

STARTUP NEEDS: To get started, Marla says you need the basics, like a business license, business cards, marketing materials and training. You also need a computer, a printer, and phone equipment. If you don't have any of these, plan on spending $500 to $1,250 for startup costs.

SKILLS NEEDED: You'll need the skills and abilities to help people develop an organizational system that will work for them, and you should be able to train them how to use the system.

MARKETING / SALES NEEDS: You can choose to focus on business clients or individual homeowners. Your value proposition is that you can really help the client with a long-term solution at an affordable rate. I don't want to pay you for a temporary fix. I want this problem to go away forever, which means the system you help me develop needs to be easy to use. Make me understand your solution is affordable and that I can continue to honor the system after you leave. Marla adds, "This is a 'people industry.' Most people are drawn to this work because they want to help others. They want to make a difference. One of the best ways to attract clients is doing as much public speaking as possible. This is how I built my business – speaking at least once a month somewhere in my community. When people hear you speak, they trust you."

HOUSEKEEPER

Have you ever thought about cleaning houses to make money? Many housekeepers have a few clients they care for on a weekly or monthly basis, meaning they earn recurring income. With enough clients, housekeepers can make significant money. Partnering with other housekeepers to keep up with demand can also add income.

Housekeeping is a great business that allows you to set your own schedule and be as busy as you want. Customers have to trust you in the intimate parts of their home and life, even when they are not there. If you earn their trust, you can be as busy as you want to be, because they'll refer business to you.

Housekeeping is a great business that allows you to set your own schedule and be as busy as you want.

The job is relatively simple. You go into someone's house and clean stuff they don't want to. You might clean only bathrooms and floors, or it could be more involved. Specify the expectations up front, so you can quote the job appropriately. I know plenty of homeowners and business owners who would gladly turn cleaning over to someone else if the price was right because they are "done" with it.

After college, I worked for a company that was started a few decades earlier. The owner of the company, Don Aslett, was a student at the local university who earned money by walking around town carrying a bucket and soap to clean houses. That was the beginning of a business that grew past $200 million in annual revenues. A cleaning business can stay as small as you want, or it has the potential to grow as big as you can dream.

Mirinda Losee, who had a housekeeping business for a year, shared her success tips with me. To get going, she says, "Start with someone you can trust, like a neighbor, friend, or relative of a friend. When Aunt Sally's bingo buddy needs some cleaning now that her husband has passed away, you're probably going to be the first choice. A personal relationship is key to enjoying your work and getting a better price for it."

She continues, "A common misconception about house cleaning is that you have to be really desperate to start a cleaning company."

Here are Mirinda's tips on pricing: Make sure your referrals know that not all jobs are the same and one price does not fit all jobs. A house that is always picked up and generally clean is going to be priced different than a home that is so untidy you can't get to the sink to clean it.

She cautions, "A big pitfall is letting your client get too comfortable with your arrangement. If you feel you need a raise because the client had a baby and it really is harder to clean up after another kid, or the client has taken up fishing and the bathroom always looks like a duck pond, it's time to move on or consider a pay increase. Don't be afraid to let your clients know what is expected of them so you can do your job properly."

Mirinda advises that if you get paid by the hour, negotiate to keep that amount consistent even if you get the same job done in less time. You'll make more money per hour as you become more efficient.

She concludes, "If you like to clean, enjoy being your own boss and could stand to get out of the house for a few hours, this might be a good part time job for you. It can be a successful business if you treat it as a successful business."

INSPIRED BY: Mirinda Losee.

EARNING POTENTIAL: Twenty dollars or more per hour.

SEASONAL: No.

LICENSE REQUIRED: No.

LEGAL CONSIDERATIONS: Incorporate. You'll be working in and around other people's personal property.

SAFETY CONSIDERATIONS: You'll be knee deep in chemicals. Gloves and masks could help, but if the chemicals irritate you too much, you might have to pursue a different business. Mirinda emphasizes working only where you are comfortable.

LOCAL REGULATIONS: Check with your city.

STARTUP COSTS: Less than one hundred dollars.

STARTUP NEEDS: You'll need cleaning supplies including chemicals, rags, and buckets. Reliable transportation is a must. Mirinda suggests that your client might provide the supplies and tools, at your recommendation. She adds, "Don't be conned into buying the most expensive products. Vinegar is your best friend in this business."

SKILLS NEEDED: Ability to work alone, persistence, and attention to detail. Although you should learn a lot on the job, you should have some knowledge of cleaning techniques and chemicals. You can also learn from the staff where you buy cleaning supplies.

MARKETING / SALES NEEDS: Mirinda says, "Referrals are definitely the way to go! Your clients will typically be homeowners, and the best way to reach them might be through word of mouth and social tools, especially Facebook. When your clients trust and like you, ask them for referrals. There is a lot of competition in this business, but there is a lot of work to do. I want to hire someone who is dependable, trustworthy, and long term. If you can position yourself as that person, and take care of your clients, they should be happy to recommend you to their friends and family. Get business cards and be proud of what you do for people because you are solving one of their daily problems!"

Lawn Care Aerator

As a homeowner, I'm continually working to keep my lawn looking decent. Some of my neighbors are retired and have plenty of time to work on their lawns, but I don't. It may sound trivial but I stress about having a yard that's good enough. In addition, I don't want my yard to be unhealthy. I mow. I spray. I fertilize. And for the first few years, I was told to aerate the lawn.

Aeration is a process where a machine pulls up small tube-sized sections of dirt to prevent the dirt from getting too packed, allowing the grass roots to get the nutrition they need. It's a basic step you take to provide a healthy environment for the grass to grow.

Starting an aerating business is relatively easy. You simply need an aerator and customers. You can spend a few hundred dollars or a few thousand dollars for an aerator. There are many models online for around $750. Just like a lawn mower, you walk it all over the lawn. It's a fast process and a lawn could be finished in about thirty minutes. I pay my aerator serviceman thirty dollars each time he aerates, once in the spring and once in the fall. He works part time and told me he can make an easy $10,000 a year as extra income.

"To be successful at this," says Tommy, "You'll want to plan on very long, labor-intensive hours each day for a month and a half. I work very long days, and drop about twenty pounds throughout the season. The aerating seasons do not last long, so to make the money I want to make, I need to be dedicated. I have to emphasize 'labor intensive,' as these machines move a lot faster than a lawn mower and demand endurance and strength to operate all day, every day during the season."

He continues, "My biggest mistake when I started was not realizing the social skills needed to do door-to-door sales. You need the right personality. If you aren't comfortable doing sales, find someone who is."

Aerating is one of those businesses that gets you outdoors. If you hustle, you can make a lot of money per hour. It isn't right for everyone but some people might really thrive in this environment.

INSPIRED BY: Tommy Thompson, my aerator.

EARNING POTENTIAL: $10,000 or more per year.

SEASONAL: Yes. Typically, aerating is done twice a year, once in the spring and once in the fall. You can do it in the summer. Before you start, you'll want to research the right times to aerate in your area.

LICENSE REQUIRED: If you go door to door, you'll need a solicitor's license.

LEGAL CONSIDERATIONS: Have the right business entity and insurance in place in case there is legal action resulting from a ruined sprinkler system or landscaping.

SAFETY CONSIDERATIONS: You'll be working with a heavy machine that you'll need to transport. You'll do a lot of walking so make sure you have comfortable footwear. Any moving machine has danger hazards. Be careful, understand the machine, and establish a safe loading/unloading process.

LOCAL REGULATIONS: Check with your city.

STARTUP COSTS: $750 to $3,000 for an aerator and a trailer to transport it to the job site.

STARTUP NEEDS: Unless you only work yards within walking distance, you'll need a vehicle for carrying the aerator or towing the trailer. However, walking an aerator around the neighborhood can be inconvenient and waste a lot of time.

SKILLS NEEDED: This is a great business for building a repeat customer base, so use a good customer relationship management tool to track and schedule semi-yearly visits. A friendly attitude will go a long way, but you need to get in, do the job, and move on to the next one. You don't get paid for extended visits.

MARKETING / SALES NEEDS: Door-to-door sales and word of mouth. This is a localized business, assuming you don't want to travel hours for just one client. Prices are relatively low (thirty dollars per yard where I live), the need is high, and the yards are plentiful. If you hit the prospect at the right time, and if they don't have an aerator already, this should be a relatively easy sale.

Mobile Head Lice Remover

I remember getting sent home from elementary school one day with an embarrassing diagnosis from the school nurse: head lice! Yuck! Honestly though, since I spent most of my time outdoors, I'm surprised I didn't get lice, fleas, and ticks more often!

When you have head lice in the public school system, you are not allowed back to school until you are lice free. Do-it-yourself cleaning can be involved, messy, and uncomfortable. This problem presents an opportunity for entrepreneurs.

As a head lice removal specialist, you help kids get lice free so they can go back to school. This can be a fun, rewarding, and exciting business. You aren't trapped in an office, and you get to meet lots of people. Parents are anxious to get rid of the problem so their kid can return to school. They are in emergency mode, which directly correlates to the amount of money you can charge.

Here are some tips from Amy Goldreyer, who has a head lice removal business in Southern California: Start small, and get clients to recommend you to others. Word of mouth is really important, as is a good website. She adds, "You need to be extremely nice to everybody, even though people will not always be nice to you. And you need to be reliable. Show up when you say you are going to show up."

As your business grows, you might need to bring in help. Amy suggests, "If you are hiring others to help you, make sure you know them really well. The people you hire will represent you and your business and could have a significant impact on any word-of-mouth advertising."

This can be a lucrative business, but not necessarily an easy one. Amy says, "Sometimes, you won't have any time to yourself. I get calls at midnight and six in the morning. Be prepared to be on call 24/7. I have had to get out of bed at 10 p.m. to treat someone because I didn't want to lose the client. You have to prioritize what you are willing to give up for a client. I realize now that owning my own business means I work way more hours than when I had a nine-to-five job. I answer phones until ten in the evening. I answer the phones on weekends and holidays. It's probably more work than a traditional job, but at least I only answer to myself, and I can choose to lose a client so I can go to my kid's concert if that's what I think is more important."

What about the actual process of removing lice? Amy says, "The biggest pitfall for anyone starting this business is thinking it's easy to remove lice. It isn't! Even experienced people run up against stubborn cases, and you need to set aside enough time to deal with the more difficult cases like super curly hair or really long hair."

Dealing with customers is very important. Amy says, "You need to be really good with children, since they bring home the lice. The parents are happy to see you, but the children are not! I once had a child pinch me really hard when the mom walked out of the room. You need to know how to deal with that. I just said very quietly to the child, 'What do you think your mom would say if I told her you just did that?' And the kid didn't touch me again."

Is this an easy business to start? Yes. But Amy cautions, "This business is something everyone thinks they can do, so there is a lot of competition. Separate yourself from the pack since there are so many lice removal companies out there."

She continues, "Beware of business review websites. I have a lot of great reviews on Yelp, but they're filtered because Yelp puts up reviews by people who review the most. So great reviews don't always show up. We have had to post all our good reviews on my website since Yelp won't post them all." This is good advice for any testimonials you receive.

Whether on social media, in an email, or in a letter, post testimonials and reviews on your own website where you can control them.

INSPIRED BY: Amy Goldreyer, HairWhisperers.com.

EARNING POTENTIAL: Forty to one hundred dollars plus per hour.

SEASONAL: No, although you might be busiest when school is in session.

LICENSE REQUIRED: Maybe.

LEGAL CONSIDERATIONS: Incorporate.

SAFETY CONSIDERATIONS: I asked Amy about chemicals. She replied, "Most lice removal companies don't use chemicals, and they don't work. You wouldn't need to hire someone to apply the chemicals because you can do that yourself."

LOCAL REGULATIONS: Check with your state licensing division. Search for "[state] license" or "[state] department of commerce."

STARTUP COSTS: Less than $250.

STARTUP NEEDS: You need a vehicle, lice removal tools, combs, drapes, and other supplies. You need billing forms and you should consider alternative method for taking payments. A cell phone and GPS will come in handy as you travel to unfamiliar areas.

SKILLS NEEDED: You should be friendly and respectful with people. This is a high-touch environment with children. As your business grows, you'll need to work effectively on a tight schedule.

MARKETING / SALES NEEDS: Develop relationships with pharmacists, school nurses, parent teacher organizations, and others parents who would ask for help. Help your clients become word-of-mouth evangelists to their friends and neighbors. Have a website that people can find easily. Amy cautions, "The worst marketing idea was advertising in parent magazines. I never got any calls from readers and it was extremely expensive. The best marketing is always word of mouth, and getting in with the schools in your area."

PERSONAL FASHION SHOPPER

I am amazed at the number of people who have been blessed with a good fashion sense. I am not one of them! The only time I like buying clothes for myself is when I find them on the 80 percent clearance rack. And let's face it, there's a reason those clothes are 80 percent off!

My best clothes used to be "hand me downs" from my brother, who has much better taste in clothes than I do. The best clothes I have now are clothes I got when shopping with my personal clothing shopper. These are the clothes I wear for my public speaking engagements.

How did I find a personal shopper? I was getting ready for my next presentation during a speaking tour in Silicon Valley. I asked my publisher if there was a clothing store I could get to before my next presentation. He immediately sent me out the door with his wife who he said "likes to help people shop for clothes."

That was an understatement. This woman was a shopping genius. As we drove from store to store, she quizzed me on my likes, dislikes and budget. Every piece of clothing she put in front of me at the store was good, and with my feedback, she got closer to what we thought would look great on me. By the end of our whirlwind shopping spree, I had three new sets of clothes that made me feel great. Thanks to this patient lady, I am no longer self conscious when I stand in front of hundreds of people.

If I knew the peace of mind I would have after shopping with her, I might have paid her $500 for solving my problem that afternoon. Does that sound like a lot of money for a couple of hours together? She spent about two hours with me, but she solved a serious problem. When I get ready for presentations now, I can confidently pack the right clothes, and feel good about what I wear to meetings. Worrying about my wardrobe sometimes interfered with my ability to do my job as a speaker.

Diana Jennings, a professional image consultant, says, “The profession of shopping for, and dressing, others is more complex than people realize. Understanding the differences in related fields will help you determine the best investment of your time and money when it comes to training, networking and marketing your business.”

She continues, “Personal shoppers work for a specific clothing retailer and select garments based on the inventory on hand. Others simply love fashion and shop for an elite clientele who have the resources to pay for a service they do not have the time to do themselves. Selections are typically based on an immediate need, the individual’s style preferences, and budget. Working as a personal shopper for a retailer is good experience while you acquire image management related skills.”

Diana elaborates, “Traditional stylists are focused on current trends, anticipate the next fad, and dress their clients in what’s hot at the moment for a photo shoot or special event. They create an image for presenting the client to the world. Stylists typically dress models for the runway, print media and work with celebrities and commercial or fashion photographers.”

She concludes, “Image consultants provide a wide range of services, and their knowledge requires depth and breadth to be credible in the field. They focus on helping clients manage their image and the perception of others through non-verbal communication. The services provided by an image consultant include, but are not limited to, those of a personal shopper and stylist. The image consultant takes on the role of an educator when working with clients.”

Diana shares some success tips:

- Avoid doing it all at once. Develop a foundation in a couple of skills and disciplines before moving on to the next. Focus energy and resources on those things that align with your ideal client and brand.

- Establish yourself as an expert. Clients are referred, or find you by doing a Google search. They have been known to take action after reading Diana's blog, subscribing to her newsletter or because the newsletter was forwarded to them by someone else. Diana explains, "Clients hire me after attending one of my programs, or after reading one of my articles. Sometimes clients receive my services as a gift or as part of professional development training. In the future, I plan to attract additional clients by writing a book."
- Manage your time carefully. If your time and energy are divided between running a household and raising children, make sure you have a good support system at home.
- Work with a mentor or coach. Getting help starting out will ensure your foray into fashion consulting doesn't fail.

I guarantee there are men and women out there with the same problem I had. Can you help them?

INSPIRED BY: My publisher's wife, Alex Levy, and Diana Jennings, brandyouimage.com.

EARNING POTENTIAL: Fifty to $300 per hour, depending on where you live, your clientele, and your experience and credentials.

SEASONAL: No.

LICENSE REQUIRED: No. Consider a certification from the Association of Image Consultants International (aica.org).

LEGAL CONSIDERATIONS: Incorporate. Diana says, "If client appointments are conducted in your office or home, or you plan to drive the client to stores, make sure you have the proper liability insurance. Consultants who provide corporate services might consider an errors and omissions insurance policy. 'E & O' insurance is designed to cover your consulting business if a client claims that your recommendations are directly responsible for a financial loss."

SAFETY CONSIDERATIONS: None.

LOCAL REGULATIONS: Check with your city.

STARTUP COSTS: Zero to thousands. Diana explains, “In-depth training runs from $3,500 to $6,000. Advanced training in color and etiquette is additional and does not include the tools necessary to properly conduct certain services, such as color analysis.”

STARTUP NEEDS: A computer, website, business cards, and training are advised, but you could wait until after you land your first few customers, especially if you start with your own network.

SKILLS NEEDED: You must have a good fashion sense, knowledge of what compliments various body types, good listening skills, patience, excellent time management skills, and a warm personality. Diana suggests a lot of training.

MARKETING / SALES NEEDS: These services are for a niche audience. Aside from the usual marketing tactics, network with other professionals at business meetings. Consider doing makeovers and presentations as lead-generating activities.

Personal Trainer

I was a gym rat in high school, spending two hours a day at the gym. Unfortunately, I didn't eat right so I didn't see the results I thought I should see. But I fell in love with the gym. I loved everything from the culture to the people to working out.

In a gym, personal trainers help people one on one. Trainers establish a good exercise plan for clients and teach them how to use the gym equipment correctly. A personal trainer will be with you when you work out, watch your form, give you advice, and answer questions. They help you understand why you are (or aren't) getting results, and can even provide nutritional guidance.

Do you love helping people? Do you love fitness and nutrition? A career as a personal trainer could be a great way for you to monetize your passions.

But wait! What if you don't look like a personal trainer?

Personal trainer Danielle Raulinaitis says, "People might assume personal trainers need to have a certain body type. I clearly don't have the best body in the gym. That is not my focus. My focus is the connection I make with a client so I can teach and motivate them on an individual level. How boring would the world be if we were all built the same?!"

A friend of mine is a fitness nut. Any morning I get to the gym before nine, he is there for his morning workout. We've talked about what he could do with this passion. He's not as interested in being a one-on-one personal trainer as he is helping companies develop and implement corporate fitness programs. Pursuing such a path might include creating a program (in the form of a book or workbook), conducting seminars onsite with employees, or setting up customized fitness programs for individuals.

There are many reasons a company would pay for fitness services. Healthier employees keep health insurance costs down. Healthier employees are more productive. Offering a perk like this might help employees feel appreciated, improving retention and staff loyalty.

Danielle says, "Companies that are smart enough to have a wellness program often don't put enough emphasis on personal trainers. There may be incentives and goals, but in order to see real results employees need to be meeting with a trainer individually. Though it may be only one session, the personal trainer should be able to provide plenty of tools that would yield endless results."

Can you communicate the added value a personal trainer could bring to an existing wellness program? If so, you can brand yourself as the missing piece.

Danielle shares, "To be successful as a personal trainer, find your niche. What is your focus and how has your history built that foundation? For example, my emphasis is on weight loss and triathlon training. Both have gotten me where I am today and I am thrilled to share and teach that to others because of my own weight loss journey and triathlon racing."

INSPIRED BY: Danielle Raulinaitis, personal trainer and triathlon athlete/enthusiast, facebook.com/pages/Rauli-Fitness-LLC/166446076786036.

EARNING POTENTIAL: Twenty-five dollars or more per hour per client, up to thousands for a corporate fitness program.

SEASONAL: No, although New Year's resolutions might help increase your business.

LICENSE REQUIRED: Danielle urges those interested in personal training to pursue a nationally recognized certification along with cardio pulmonary resuscitation (CPR) and automated external defibrillator (AED) training. A state business license may be required if you're a contractor and not an employee of the gym.

LEGAL CONSIDERATIONS: Incorporate.

SAFETY CONSIDERATIONS: You should have enough safety training to help your clients, whether they are working on gym machines or dealing with their own health problems.

LOCAL REGULATIONS: None.

STARTUP COSTS: Zero to thousands.

STARTUP NEEDS: You should have nice gym clothes to project a professional and competent image. Enthusiasm for, and knowledge of, fitness, nutrition and workout safety are also are essential.

SKILLS NEEDED: You should have a good knowledge of the gym equipment and an understanding of current training techniques. You should be able to communicate well with people who might be intimidated and nervous. Danielle says a good personal trainer has to be a motivator and an educator to help clients achieve their desired results.

MARKETING / SALES NEEDS: Whether you are prospecting an individual or a company, you'll need to be perceived as an expert, and be able to communicate that. Look for referral partners who can recommend you, like the people at the gym's front desk, or someone who provides benefits to companies. Network with other personal trainers who might refer clients to you because their schedules are fully booked.

Spin Instructor

Isn't it crazy that some people make money doing what they used to pay to do, for fun or as a hobby? As I learned from Ann Belliveau Iacoboni in Minnesota, opportunities to monetize are endless. Ann is an exercise enthusiast who became a certified spin instructor. But spinning is a part-time gig for her. During the day, she is a business analyst for a large company. As a spin instructor, Ann gets to schedule time to take care of herself, socialize, and enjoy sharing her passion with others while earning money.

Before you get too excited thinking you will be paid to work out, consider Ann's advice: The mindset of "hey, I can get paid to work out" doesn't work. You need to engage with people in your classes. Know who they are and talk with them after class. If you want to succeed, do what you can to bring in new students and keep them coming back.

Ann is paid five dollars per person, per class. She could make $200 in a day, depending on how many people come to her classes and how many classes she teaches. If she teaches one class weekly, she could earn an extra $800 per month. However, Ann notes, "If you are an independent instructor, some factors like the scheduled time for your classes or an increase in fees may be out of your control. These things can impact your potential income."

If Ann lost her corporate job and pursued spinning full time, she believes she could make between $50,000 and $100,000 annually, especially if she had her own studio.

A studio could be used by other instructors, which means she could lease the space out for other classes and to independent personal trainers. This would give her more billable hours during the day. Of course, she wouldn't instruct spinners eight hours a day, even if she had her own studio! She might bring in other instructors to teach different types of classes. If she had her own studio, or leased space at another studio, she could make more than five dollars per student, even if she wasn't the instructor.

Getting to that point in her business would take a lot of work. Ann would need to find a venue to lease. Then she would need to market her classes, competing with local gyms and existing spin classes. She would have to buy the right insurance and check for any local regulations applying to gyms or similar businesses. She would have to create signup forms and develop payment processing. Any of these challenges might be big enough to scare people off, but if it means you are more empowered with your finances, it might be worth it.

Ann recommends talking with different clubs to find out how their instructors are compensated. "The club where I teach pays per spinner," Ann explains, "So you want to get as many spinners in your class as possible. Volunteer to substitute for other instructors so the spinners in those classes can experience your spin style. Get business cards made with the places you teach and hand them out."

Spinning is an intense workout, but the people in the class can have a lot of fun and meet new friends. What a great work environment!

INSPIRED BY: Ann Belliveau Iacoboni, spin instructor in Minnesota.

EARNING POTENTIAL: Hundreds to thousands per month.

SEASONAL: No, although New Year's resolutions might impact your business.

LICENSE REQUIRED: No, but certifications will make you more credible. Ann advises, "Talk with instructors, especially the ones you really like. Ask them where they were certified."

LEGAL CONSIDERATIONS: If you are in a gym or someone else's studio, make sure they have the right legal protection that covers you as a subcontractor. If it is your own studio, consult an attorney or insurance agent to ensure you are properly covered.

SAFETY CONSIDERATIONS: You need to be healthy enough to endure the workouts and talk with people after the session. If you aren't ready now, you will likely build up your endurance!

Corporate Trainer

This is one of two ideas that inspired me to write this book. While on a speaking tour in Silicon Valley, I was able to sit down at a coffee shop with Rosemary Mark, who has one of the coolest jobs in the world. She invents recipes for companies. I have always loved to cook and create things in the kitchen. Sitting across the table from someone who does this professionally was a treat!

Rosemary asked me for a consulting session to talk about her personal brand. During the course of our discussion, I had an idea for her that would marry her skills and passion in the kitchen with my recent experience as a professional speaker. I asked her if she could combine her cooking experience with her background as a presenter to create a revenue stream providing services as a corporate trainer.

She replied, "I already know plenty of people who do that type of thing." She didn't sound hopeful, even though she had everything she needed to make money doing this. Her perception was that the market already had plenty of people who did corporate training in a kitchen. The people she knew would bring an audience into a kitchen where they would break into small teams to cook something. However, my idea was different.

I suggested something rather bold. Rosemary could brand herself as a corporate trainer who cooks in front of her audience, instead using the participants to cook. She could choose from many in-demand topics such as teamwork, creativity or leadership, and create an engaging presentation while sharing points illustrated through the preparation process. Instead of involving the audience in the cooking process, my idea was that she would present a program similar to a TV cooking show. Splitting your audience into three-person teams sounded like the perfect recipe for losing attention to conversations. Instead, she would present and cook in such a way that she would capture everyone's attention, and entertain them as she illustrates principles from the topic. It would create more entertainment while managing the audience's focus and attention.

This Alternative would fill the need to convey important and relevant corporate training in an engaging and memorable way. We've all attended boring corporate training events. Boring means I can't wait to get out of there, and I'm not interested in the content. The "packaging" or presentation style could be as important as the material. A dry presentation makes us wonder when we can leave to look for that important email we're expecting. This type of presentation could be engaging and fun, providing the audience with information to think about and discuss with their team.

I knew Rosemary could take traditional corporate training to a different level. Her presentation might be titled "Seven Ingredients Every Team Needs" or "Turn Up the Heat on Your Creative Juices." She could easily create a two-hour seminar on each topic that illustrates different learning objectives reinforced by experiences for all five senses: smell, touch, sight, feel and even hearing.

In her presentation, Rosemary could show things with food that might seem magical. At my suggestion, she replied, "Did you know that you can mix oil and vinegar? All you need is a little mustard." This made me think of a team that isn't working well together . . . it just needs one more ingredient to make the mix work! This is just one example of how her presentation could introduce a different perspective about challenges with teamwork, creativity, or whatever the topic is. Her audience would follow along with her charming presentation to see what she's going to do next, while learning how they could do their job better.

Because I've done training and speaking, I know companies would pay top dollar. I told Rosemary she could probably charge between

$2,000 and $5,000 per presentation, and work her way up to $10,000 per presentation. Because she is within driving distance to many target companies, she could keep her calendar as full as she wants without ever getting on a plane.

If you make $10,000 per presentation, you could run this business and only work one day each month! Of course, there is preparation and cleanup time, and you need to schedule time to develop your presentation, but this is serious money. Rosemary has a competitive edge that could make her very unique amongst competitors in this space.

If you make ten thousand dollars per presentation, you could run this business and only work one day a month!

Could you take your passion and expertise and position yourself uniquely as a special trainer for corporate audiences? To get the feedback you need, you could brainstorm a list of ideas and ask friends who work in a corporate environment to introduce you to the appropriate people. You might already have what it takes to make this a successful revenue stream.

INSPIRED BY: Rosemary Mark, RosemayMark.com.

EARNING POTENTIAL: Thousands of dollars per engagement.

SEASONAL: No.

LICENSE REQUIRED: No.

LEGAL CONSIDERATIONS: Incorporate.

SAFETY CONSIDERATIONS: Ensure the area is appropriate for preparing food in front of an audience. You don't want the effects of your presentation superseded by the news that everyone got food poisoning.

LOCAL REGULATIONS: If you are using the host company's kitchen, you should be fine. Check to see if it is set up for food preparation.

STARTUP COSTS: None, assuming you have equipment and you will use the host company's facility.

STARTUP NEEDS: To start my training and speaking career, I simply needed nice clothes. If you were to start a business like this, you would need all the cooking supplies required for your presentation and those items will depend on your topic, style and audience.

SKILLS NEEDED: You should have a strong message and be able to present well. If you have an incapacitating fear of public speaking, you'll need to get over it by getting training. You should be organized enough to appear professional before, during, and after the presentation, especially since each presentation might be like a laboratory experiment where things can go wrong. The kitchen might be where you are comfortable, but you'll also have to manage the business side such as negotiating contracts and invoicing. Be prepared to deal with corporate clients that have tedious contract and collection policies.

MARKETING / SALES NEEDS: Network with managers, internal trainers, human resources staff and training companies who purchase training from vendors. Get in front of the decision makers at your target companies. Make it easy for others to talk about you by branding yourself as a unique corporate trainer. I suggested that Rosemary do this type of training in her own kitchen for her neighbors and ask her guests to spread the word amongst their business contacts. Once you develop a witty, highly entertaining brand, encourage others to talk about you and get introductions. If you're the best trainer they've brought in all year, they should be happy to share your name with industry colleagues.

Project Management Consultant

Because I run a software company, I continually have project management needs. When I work on big book projects, go out on the road for a speaking tour, or something else that takes me away from JibberJobber for days or weeks at a time, other projects tend to get neglected. Some projects are big, long term, and require my attention for months or years. Other projects are small and unusual with a higher learning curve.

Anyone who has done project management knows that doing it well is very time consuming. If I could offload even a portion of the projects I manage, I would be able to focus on important elements such as growth and strategy. If you have project management skills, this is where your supply meets my demand. Can you help me?

As a project management consultant, you need to effectively communicate your value to me. You are not necessarily asking for a job or a long-term commitment. You might even position yourself as my executive administrator with the ability to correctly complete my projects so I can focus on other things.

Many of you have project management experience. Some of you are certified project managers. If you can help me finish my projects, you can significantly impact my business. Even though I know I need to get them done, I have been putting off some projects for years. Some new projects are high priority, but I just don't have the mental bandwidth to complete them.

Certified Project Management Professional Wayne Parris advises aspiring consultants, "Make sure you understand what it is you want to do. Are you creating a business or a practice? A business will go on even when you're not there. A practice relies solely on you. It's like being a doctor. If you don't see patients, you don't get paid and no one can do it for you. Take the time to put together a business plan that covers the four Ps of marketing: Product (or service), Pricing, Placement, and Promotion. This forces you to think about and make choices regarding what you are doing and how you're going to do it. Who is your customer? Where are they? How are you going to reach them? How do they know about your services? What are you going to charge? Will you charge hourly or per project? Find a business plan template and start filling it out. It will generate a lot of questions that require answers."

He continues, "If you can't describe what you do on paper, how are you going to describe it on the fly? Isn't that what we try to do with project management? Don't we describe a reasonably assembled schedule that delineates how to get from A to B?"

To be successful, Wayne says you need three things: focus, perseverance and hard work. He explains, "Make sure you know who your customers are and focus on them, not on chasing the next dollar. Make sure you understand the nature of the work you wish to pursue. Don't try to be all things to all people. They can see right through that."

Wayne talks about a common challenge entrepreneurs face. He says you need "sufficient capital to grow your business into a self-sustaining entity, which happens when you have a large enough customer base that keeps you busy full time. This means building a nest egg while you're searching for customers."

He continues, "The other pitfall is when you're a stand-alone consultant. It's either feast or famine. When you're working, you typically aren't marketing or lining up the next job. Then, when your assignment ends, you begin searching for the next project. It can be difficult to roll right off one job onto another. If you're used to a steady paycheck, you have to learn to save up to make it through the times when you're not working."

I guarantee there are many busy executives and business owners who have a considerable load to carry. Having someone take on certain projects could be a great help to them. Whether you are a very specialized software project manager or can help with any kind of project, such as presentations, speeches, and other tasks, you could add structure and process to a client's schedule that would make them more effective and productive.

INSPIRED BY: Wayne Parris, All3pm.com.

EARNING POTENTIAL: Wayne says, "In general, consulting feeds could run fifty to $200 per hour depending on expertise, length of contract, and other factors."

SEASONAL: No.

LICENSE REQUIRED: No.

LEGAL CONSIDERATIONS: Incorporate.

SAFETY CONSIDERATIONS: None.

LOCAL REGULATIONS: None.

STARTUP COSTS: None.

STARTUP NEEDS: You'll need a phone and a computer. Transportation to client's location may be necessary as well.

SKILLS NEEDED: You should be able to stay very organized and learn quickly. You will need to execute on plans and schedules, and probably manage different people who are key to getting the jobs done. You will likely negotiate and communicate regularly with service providers and "stakeholders."

MARKETING / SALES NEEDS: Recognize and easily communicate your value proposition to your target audience so they can understand why they should hire you. Wayne says, "You need to be seen as an expert. Start a website. Send out a newsletter. Speak at conferences. Write white papers. Be the go-to expert people need to solve their particular kind of problem."

He adds, "The best marketing strategy for me is the PMI (Project Management Institute) career website where you can upload your resume for others to find and peruse. People looking for project managers go to a project management website."

Presentation Trainer/Coach

I typically get very positive feedback after I speak. I'm sometimes asked if I have received professional training. Although I pay attention to feedback and advice so I can improve as a speaker, I have never been professionally trained. I regularly critique other speakers, making notes of things to emulate as well as things to never do.

I have chosen to be a professional speaker, so this is my craft. I work on it, just as you work on yours. I have tricks, tactics and strategies. If I were a presentation trainer, I could teach you my tricks, tactics and strategies . . . for the right price.

The market for presentation training is huge because it includes anyone who needs to make a presentation. For example, someone who might have their job or promotion on the line might need to prepare for a board presentation. Chief executive officers routinely need to present to prospective customers. A Master of Business Administration candidate needs to defend her thesis in front of a board or panel before she is awarded her degree. The possibilities are endless: speakers at a conference or networking event, business owners pitching to venture capitalists, salespeople, and even professional trainers.

That's where you come in. You could offer individual and group coaching to help people give presentations with more impact. You can coach on using visual aids, appearance and dress, body language, delivery and projection, style, jokes, timing and other techniques.

If you present well, or can coach someone on presenting well, maybe you can make money using your skills. How much money? Professional speaking coach Lisa Braithwaite says, "For an individual client, I charge $600 for three hours of coaching. Training engagements vary by the level of customization, but for a full day of training, I charge around $3,000. I also offer other speaking-related services such as PowerPoint design."

Lisa has defined her own niche audience. She shares her philosophy, "It's important to have your own philosophy of public speaking and coaching and figure out what sets you apart. Why should someone hire you? What do you have that other coaches don't have? The people who are attracted to me are the people I'm trying to attract. My style is informal, conversational and not rules based, and this is what I teach. People who seek me out aren't looking for a corporate, buttoned-down type of coach. Figure out who you are in the public speaking universe, what you have to say, and who you want to hear it. Be willing to stand up for your own beliefs and opinions and rock the boat if necessary."

A typical day for Lisa might involve any or all of these tasks: marketing, writing a blog post or her newsletter, working on a book, researching, presentations or client work, creating information products, updating her website, submitting speaker proposals, and in-person networking. A chunk of her day might be spent on individual coaching or completing a client project like designing a PowerPoint or editing a video. She might have a speaking or training engagement, or attend a conference.

I love how Lisa talks about her clients, "Most of my clients are pleasant to work with. I have had very few demanding or troublesome clients and, so far, I haven't wanted to fire anyone. For the most part, they are motivated to improve and are willing to do what it takes."

INSPIRED BY: Lisa Braithwaite, CoachLisaB.com.

EARNING POTENTIAL: At least $500 per client.

SEASONAL: No.

LICENSE REQUIRED: No.

LEGAL CONSIDERATIONS: Incorporate.

SAFETY CONSIDERATIONS: None.

LOCAL REGULATIONS: None.

STARTUP COSTS: None.

STARTUP NEEDS: You don't need anything special to start this business.

SKILLS NEEDED: You should know how to present well enough to coach people. An excellent presenter doesn't necessarily make an excellent coach, and vice versa. As a coach, you'll need to be assertive as you coach your client on how to improve their presentation.

MARKETING/SALES NEEDS: Define your niche audience and aggressively market to that audience. Be where your audience is, network, and clearly brand yourself as the expert who can help them communicate more effectively. Lisa elaborates, "My target market includes entrepreneurs and professionals. I do a lot of online marketing through my blog, website, and social media. This works great for me and keeps me at the top of a Google search. It also requires a large time investment. I do a lot of in-person networking locally. I've had very little success with paid advertising and directories."

SAFETY/SECURITY INSPECTOR

How much money does a safety or environmental accident cost a company? The cost can easily run billions of dollars and can include government fines, lost sales, cleanup, and fixing damaged public perception. Safety or environmental issues could destroy companies and careers, and hurt families and communities. Safety issues could bring a life to a tragic end.

That's where someone like Craig Klein comes in. For almost twenty years, Craig has been conducting safety and environmental audits, assessments, and consulting on environmental issues. Based on his experience and reputation, Craig is able to offer his services as a consultant to companies of all sizes. He may be brought in as a reaction to an accident, or he might be hired as part of a proactive annual audit. His job is to help a company understand and document safety concerns, and help them make necessary adjustments to prevent problems.

In the safety and environmental space, your clients could be large companies or organizations such as oil companies, governments, landlords, and manufacturing plants. You might service small companies that are setting up facilities or processes. Your assistance and expertise will be needed in complying with proper safety practices. Some of your revenue will come from one-time issues, such as responding to an emergency situation. Some of your revenue might come from performing regular safety audits, perhaps quarterly or annually. Contracts for regular audits mean less marketing, less stress, and the ability to do safety-related work instead of continually looking for new clients.

I know many of you don't have the experience in this very specialized field, but I wanted to include it in this book for two reasons. First, I know people who do have this expertise and could create a business doing this type of work. Second, what subject matter expertise do you have that people would pay you to learn? If you have very specialized experience, there is probably a market for your expertise. You might not know about the need in the market, but people are probably looking for your expertise right now. They might not be looking for a full-time employee. But if they have a problem, and you are the expert, they will pay you to solve their problem.

INSPIRED BY: Craig Klein, kleinenviro.com.

EARNING POTENTIAL: Fifty to $150 per hour, or thousands of dollars per project.

SEASONAL: No.

LICENSE REQUIRED: Check local and state regulations to see if you need a license. Consider obtaining industry certifications to establish credibility, and ensure you are trained and qualified. Craig suggests the following trainings and designations: Certified Hazardous Materials Manager (CHMM), Project Management Professional (PMP) and Certified Safety Professional (CSP).

LEGAL CONSIDERATIONS: Your reports and analysis can significantly impact operations, a company's future, and lives. Craig says, "Obtaining professional liability insurance is important."

SAFETY CONSIDERATIONS: You could regularly be in dangerous situations. Ensure you have the right equipment and proper training, such as Hazardous Waste Operations Safety Training. This is forty hours of training with additional training required each year to stay current.

LOCAL REGULATIONS: Check with your city.

STARTUP COSTS: $1,000 to $3,000.

STARTUP NEEDS: If you don't have the skills and experience required to be a safety/environmental expert, plan to spend a lot of time training and earning certifications. Not everyone has a background that prepares them to be a safety expert. If you want to do this as an independent consultant, expect to spend at least five years in the industry training, gaining experience, and earning certifications. Tools needed for some jobs (testing air, water, and other conditions) can be very expensive. You might find someone in the industry who already has the tools, licenses, certifications and customers. Consider partnering with them rather than starting your own business.

SKILLS NEEDED: This is a very technical business. Aside from safety experience and training, you will need to focus on marketing and selling your services. Many of your clients will bring you in only when your services are needed. Nurture relationships with clients and prospects since you never know when the next emergency will be, which is when you might get that call. Confidentiality is critical as you build those essential relationships. Network extensively with internal safety and environmental officers in the industry.

MARKETING / SALES NEEDS: Developing personal relationships with people in large companies is essential. Learn to network into companies and attend industry conferences. Differentiate yourself and your offering from others by writing white papers, a safety blog or a book, or by making it easy for people to give you recommendations and make introductions.

Specialty Meal Preparer

I never would have believed this if I hadn't met a guy who actually did it. My new friend, Paul Wilson, told me during lunch that he recently lost seventy pounds. And he did it, in large part, because of the person who brought him his daily meals.

Paul hired a lady who knew how to make juiced meals with enough nutrition for each day. He also took vitamins and supplements. Each morning, she left bottled meals on his porch. She made them the night before and refrigerated them, or she got up early to make them that morning.

Paul shares his story and how he found someone who solved his problem, "Before I found Meg to prepare my juices, it would take me three hours a night to juice the meals I needed for the next day. Preparing meals several days in advance took even longer. Having fresh juice was crucial to my diet, and I couldn't create a large enough batch to last a month. Three days was the maximum I could make in advance.

Due to the time commitment and my already busy schedule, I started slacking on my juicing, and my body suffered from it. My eyes sunk into their sockets and my muscles atrophied noticeably. My doctor was concerned. This sort of hardcore diet requires dedication to preparation. Meg literally saved my body and many hours of my time. She also helped me change the diet so it was healthier. Meg was worth every dollar I paid her each month."

Originally, The Juice Lady (Paul's nickname for Meg) covered the cost of purchasing the food. After a couple of weeks, Meg and Paul agreed he would reimburse her for those costs. She made decent money from either business model. Paul says he didn't mind paying for Meg's preparation time while reimbursing her for the foods she used. It meant he didn't have to go grocery shopping while juice fasting, which was another time saver.

What if The Juice Lady found five clients who needed her service? Not everyone is anxious to go on a juice-only diet, but she could make and freeze other meals. In some markets, making "fresh" food with organic recipes is a big deal. I love to cook, but many people don't want to hassle with it. Fast and easy options are usually unhealthy or expensive. Why not provide a healthy, reasonably priced alternative?

Depending on where you are, there may be a local market for daily or weekly meal preparation. If you love to cook and have the right tools and environment, this could be a fun and rewarding revenue stream.

Here are some of Paul's success tips for this type of business:

Schedule – Work with the client's schedule. Paul hired Meg because he needed someone to help him create more time in his day. If Meg had set limitations that didn't work with his schedule, he would not have continued to work with her.

Favorites – Find meals the client likes and make them more often. Meg constantly asked for feedback on her juices. She stopped making the meals Paul didn't like and made more of the meals he did.

Referrals – When he finished the diet, Meg asked Paul if he knew anyone else who could use her services. Paul spoke to a friend who was intrigued by his weight loss experience and asked him for more information. If Meg hadn't asked for referrals, Paul wouldn't have suggested his friend. That referral turned out to be a great client.

Convenience – If someone is hiring you to prepare food, it is usually for their convenience. Figure out ways to add convenience to your offering. For example, Paul gave Meg a key to his house because it was more convenient for her to stock his refrigerator than worry about juices spoiling while left on the doorstep. This freed Meg's schedule since she didn't have to deliver the bottles first thing in the morning, and it was extremely convenient for Paul.

Obviously Paul and Meg had a good customer/vendor relationship. I'm sure Meg had fun working with Paul while offering a service she was passionate about. Can you do something similar?

INSPIRED BY: Paul Wilson, MyMarketer.net.

EARNING POTENTIAL: $500 to $1,000 per month per client.

SEASONAL: No.

LICENSE REQUIRED: Check to see if there are state or local food preparation requirements.

LEGAL CONSIDERATIONS: Incorporate. One mistake could lead to disastrous results.

SAFETY CONSIDERATIONS: Since you'll be working with food, there are a number of obvious safety considerations. Make sure you deliver fresh, clean food that has been prepared in the right environment and stored in clean containers.

LOCAL REGULATIONS: Check on local food preparation regulations.

STARTUP COSTS: Less than $500.

STARTUP NEEDS: Assemble everything necessary to make the meals. Whether you are preparing juices that don't require any cooking, or you are making full meals, make sure your kitchen is properly stocked and equipped. You'll need containers for delivering the meals. If you use disposable containers, you'll have repeat costs that you should bill back to the client.

SKILLS NEEDED: You should have a passion for cooking and food preparation. The ability to plan, buy, prepare and deliver food is a must. Do not under price your service or you might not realize any profits.

MARKETING / SALES NEEDS: You want to find people who are passionate about losing weight and realize it would be easier to have someone manage their food preparation. Look for people who are busy with work and other responsibilities, or caretakers who are simply too busy. Figure out your distinct value proposition – healthy choice, locally grown produce, convenience, time saver, or easy to work with – and pitch that.

Word of mouth will be powerful as your clients undergo visible weight loss changes. Paul says, “When I finished my diet, several friends were interested in Meg's services. I was able to connect her to a wealthy politician's wife who watched my dramatic weight loss and wanted those same results. In the end, this client paid Meg three times the monthly amount I had paid her.”

Tax Preparer

You know how you love to do taxes? Here's a secret: No one else loves to do taxes! I read somewhere that people would rather cut their own hair than prepare their own taxes. As you now know, where there is pain for one person, there is opportunity for another.

The UniversalAccountingHomeTaxBusiness.com website states you can make about $7,500 during your first tax season, and as your business grows, you can expect to make between $20,000 and $30,000 during the three-month tax season.*

Preparing taxes is not easy work. Finding clients takes time, and the preparation can be tedious, even boring. Attention to detail is an absolute must. Mistakes can be costly for the tax preparer and the client, so you should be current on all required training. Your clients might be individuals or companies, both of which are different enough that you might want to service one or the other. If you do a good job, you can keep those clients for many years. Some companies file taxes quarterly, which means you will bill them at least four times during the year, not just on April 15, the date income taxes are due in the United States.

Tax preparer Stacie Bakos says, "Someone wanting to go into tax preparation should know what will be required of them." She adds, "Some people may be discouraged because it's too hard or too complicated for the average person to learn. It's just like any other learned skill. We are capable of a lot when we put our heart into it."

Stacie warns that tax laws change constantly. You have to be on top of the changes or you may incur costly fines. To help you stay on top of the changes, the IRS posts the current tax code online.

Stacie talks about servicing clients and growing a tax preparation business: Success comes from going the extra mile for your client. Take the time to save them money. You will have a loyal client because they know you care. She adds, "The best way to build a client base is by referral. Encourage this by offering a discount for referrals. Mailers are a waste of money. People trust you with their money, and a postcard can't build that trust."

INSPIRED BY: Stacie Bakos, independent tax preparer.

EARNING POTENTIAL: Stacie says, "$55,000 a year (gross)," depending on your clientele.

SEASONAL: Yes, but businesses can keep you busy throughout the year.

LICENSE REQUIRED: Stacie says, "Yes. The Internal Revenue Service (IRS) regulates tax preparation."

LEGAL CONSIDERATIONS: Stacie suggests incorporating to protect your personal liability. Protect your practice with an errors and omissions insurance policy.

SAFETY CONSIDERATIONS: None.

LOCAL REGULATIONS: Each state might have different rules for tax preparers.

STARTUP COSTS: "$993 to $2,443, plus insurance," says Stacie.

STARTUP NEEDS: The costs are broken down as follows:

- Fifteen annual hours of continuing education credits, averaging about ten dollars an hour, plus registration.
- Becoming a registered tax preparer with the IRS – $125 for the exam plus study materials.
- Tax preparer ID (PTIN) to be able to do the now-mandatory e-filing – sixty-three dollars.
- Finger print clearance card – fifty to $75.
- Software programs – between $500 and $2000.

- Errors and omissions insurance – the less experience you have the higher the premium.
- Setting up your limited liability company – fifty to $500.
- Computer, printer, telephone and transportation.

SKILLS NEEDED: You should have good computer skills, and be able to gather and analyze data. Your clients might not give you a nice, pretty package from which you can extract numbers, so you might have to investigate and question the numbers to get it right. Consider working for one of the big tax preparation companies for a season to learn what you can, and then offer your skills independently the next year.

MARKETING / SALES NEEDS: As a business owner, I need to trust you before I give you my business. I have to know you will respect my confidentiality. This is a business of trust. Show you are trustworthy as well as competent, and current on ways to save me from paying more than I should. Have business cards and make it easy for others to talk about you. Encourage your clients to ask their family and friends if they need help with their taxes. If you service businesses, network locally to make it easy for businesses to talk to their peers about your services. Just because someone already uses a tax preparer doesn't mean they are happy with them, which means you might be able to service them.

*http://www.hometaxbusiness.com/start-tax-business.html

TUTOR

I didn't have a tutor during high school but some of my friends did, and they got better grades because of those tutoring sessions. Parents are concerned about grades so their kids can get into good colleges after high school. This is where tutors come in.

Did you excel in any topics in school? As an adult, have you gained a new passion for a specific subject? Maybe your knowledge can help students get better grades.

My cousin, Jordan Willison, is in the dental program at University of Nevada Las Vegas. He told me tutoring is a great way to make money. It makes sense for a college student to make twenty dollars per hour tutoring others rather than working at a restaurant making less than ten dollars an hour. Jordan can hand pick clients who are motivated to be with him.

Jordan says, "Tutoring is an option for anyone, even if they have only completed high school. You only have to be knowledgeable in at least one subject and teach it well. Because I was a biology major in college, I teach anything related to science and testing skills. I started out charging twenty dollars an hour just to get my foot in the door and build my client base. Within a week, I raised my prices to twenty-five dollars an hour for high school tutoring and thirty dollars an hour for college students, and have stopped advertising on Craigslist."

He continues, "I think I'm in such high demand because I have a college degree and a high level of knowledge in my subject area. Even at thirty dollars an hour, I am on the low side."

Tutors will always be in demand because parents and students want to get better grades, be competitive for scholarships, and have a better chance at getting into the colleges where they want to go. Whether it's for university admissions, scholarships, or to stay on the school team, your tutoring clients will be extremely motivated. There are a number of online resources for tutors to learn about billing rates, how to get started, and review tips from other tutors.

Are you passionate about sharing knowledge and helping a student achieve more? Do you want to work with motivated high school or college students? If so, tutoring might be an excellent revenue stream for you.

What if you live in a small town or have transportation issues? An article at Inc.com* states that online tutoring is a $100 million plus industry. This opens up your options for getting clients, when and how to meet with them, and even what you can teach. To facilitate an appropriate learning environment, many online tools are free or very inexpensive. Aside from being able to service clients all over the world, you can work in your pajamas and not spend any time travelling to a client location.

INSPIRED BY: My cousin, Jordan Willison.

EARNING POTENTIAL: Twenty dollars an hour or more per hour.

SEASONAL: The traditional school year would be the busiest time but people are always in school.

LICENSE REQUIRED: No.

LEGAL CONSIDERATIONS: Incorporate.

SAFETY CONSIDERATIONS: It depends on who your students are. Whether the student is in elementary school, high school, or college, you should never be alone with the client.

LOCAL REGULATIONS: None.

STARTUP COSTS: None.

STARTUP NEEDS: It depends on the subject, but you might not need anything more than a notepad and a pencil.

SKILLS NEEDED: You should have enough training and passion about the subjects you are going to teach your clients. Your job is not to help them learn everything about the subject, but to help them understand the material and prepare to score higher on tests. Don't get overwhelmed by the scope of the topics you teach. For example, you might not be qualified to be a calculus tutor, but you might be a great sixth grade math tutor. Identify your ideal client (elementary, high school, college) and make sure your knowledge and skills align with what they need.

MARKETING / SALES NEEDS: Guidance counselors could be great referral sources. Ask for referrals from clients and parents. Let students and parents know you have open slots and you are looking for more clients. Since you don't have to be physically present with your client, you can let people know about your tutoring service through Skype and other online tools.

*http://www.entrepreneur.com/article/170786

VOCAL TEACHER

Anjanette Mickelsen is a world-class vocal coach who helps people learn to use their voices better. Before a big speaking tour, I was advised to book a session with her so she could help me use my voice the right way. I squeezed fourteen scheduled speaking engagements into a four-day trip. I had no idea how that much speaking would exhaust and stress my vocal chords. I regret not booking a session with her before I left.

Anjanette got her start when she was in high school taking voice lessons from a vocal coach. From the first session, she saw immediate results. She knew she wanted to teach voice lessons for a living. Now, Anjanette is recognized as a leading voice coach with the highest designation in the technique she teaches, which is Speech Level Singing.

Anjanette charges $150 per hour. If she bills two hours a day, she makes a nice income. As her reputation has grown, so has her client list, and she easily books more than two billable hours each day. Some days are packed full while other days are "rest days." She has control over her schedule which allows her to take personal time for herself, recharge, or work on other projects. Her clients are from all over the world, and include professional singers as well as amateurs. Teaching at international singing programs during the summer increases Anjanette's revenue and her brand awareness. She also networks at a lot of music events, and supports her clients by attending their performances.

Anjanette explains, “A common misconception is that anybody who sings well can be a singing teacher. A successful vocal coach requires multiple skill sets. Get the proper training in vocal and teaching methods. I highly recommend the Speech Level Singing Teacher Certification program where you can train in both vocal and teaching techniques.”

She continues, “Focus on building a clientele, especially as you start your business. Building a great clientele takes time and patience. It is a lot like planting seeds in a garden. You may not get immediate results but, once the plants start growing, it is well worth the effort and very rewarding.”

Anjanette talks about developing relationships, “The music business is one of relationships. Be a likeable, personable, caring person. For most people, singing is a very personal and emotional experience because your voice is a part of who you are and how you express yourself to the world. People generally don't get hurt or offended if they hear they have a crappy guitar, but it can be a very hurtful experience if they hear they have a crappy voice. One of the reasons for my success as a vocal coach is that I can genuinely help people improve even if they think they are a hopeless case. I try to be patient with every student regardless of their natural ability, or where they are in their progression. I truly believe in my students and because of the technique I teach, I KNOW I can help each one, if they are willing to do the work. I give hope to my students.”

INSPIRED BY: Anjanette Mickelsen, TheSingingPro.com.

EARNING POTENTIAL: From twenty to $150+ per hour.

SEASONAL: No.

LICENSE REQUIRED: No.

LEGAL CONSIDERATIONS: Incorporate.

SAFETY CONSIDERATIONS: Anjanette says, “Some students will need medical attention because of vocal nodules, polyps, acid reflux, allergies, and many other conditions that can affect the voice. Develop a relationship with an ear, nose and throat doctor familiar with working with singers. Voices can become permanently damaged because of poor vocal training or medical issues."

LOCAL REGULATIONS: None.

STARTUP COSTS: Zero to $1,000.

STARTUP NEEDS: This can be a no-cost business to get into, although you should budget for continuing education, associations and certification fees. Your own training will validate you as a better coach to prospects and clients. Anjanette adds, "You must have a piano or keyboard to play vocal scales for students, and a sound system such as a computer, iPod, or MP3 player to play music. I highly recommend a recording device of some kind to record the vocal lessons for students to practice with after the session. Many smart phones have apps with recording capabilities. Portable recording devices are great as well."

SKILLS NEEDED: Training in voice, singing, choir or anything related, and passion for the music business. You will train serious aspiring artists, children, and people who just want to be better for a local or church choir. You have to know your craft and know how to teach voice lessons. Working well with people and helping them realize results will help you sustain and grow your business.

MARKETING / SALES NEEDS: Network with local music organizations and local music stores to create a source of referrals. Anjanette explains, "This is a business of relationships and, word-of-mouth marketing is by far the best and fastest way to build your teaching clientele. Other methods of advertising, such as social marketing or flyers, can help but word of mouth is best. Volunteering your time and skills is a great way to meet people and spread the word about what you do."

PIANO SELLER

Richard Parkinson is a man with a musical mission. He is a professional songwriter and music producer living in Utah. More than once, he has been tempted to move to Nashville to be in the middle of songwriting activity and networking. So far, he has stayed in Utah and is now known for the numerous songwriting events he hosts.

Richard has a strong background in music. At one point in his career, he sold pianos at a piano store, and represented the store at fairs and other events. I met him when he was selling pianos at our local Costco. Because of Richard's background in music and his experience selling pianos, he can easily pick up occasional shift work at the piano store. He can work as much as he wants to, allowing him to work on his songwriting and production business while earning enough money to pay bills.

Like many businesses, songwriting takes a while to build. You can spend days, weeks, months, even years working on songs and submitting them before you earn a return. Selling pianos, however, can bring in a commission check almost immediately. If Richard wants to make an extra thousand dollars a month, he knows he just needs to spend time calling customers, networking, and prospecting at musical events

This is not a full-time job for Richard, allowing flexibility in his schedule. He could probably work more hours than he does. There are opportunities to represent the piano store at special events, and he has to be available or he will miss the commission opportunity. This is flexible enough that he can still work on his other revenue streams. Richard's specialties, passion and experience make him an ideal piano salesperson. When he plays a piano in front of prospects, they get excited about the sound he creates, and hope someone in their family can do the same thing. Richard becomes a friend and fellow piano-enthusiast, not a salesperson. Do you have specialties, passion or experience that identifies you as an ideal salesperson? Are you passionate about flowers and gardening? Are you passionate about home construction, stereo systems or ponds? If you can get excited about building, creating, learning, or the end product of something, maybe you can share your excitement and knowledge with others who will buy. That's what this Alternative is about.

INSPIRED BY: Richard Parkinson, OneRichSong.com.

EARNING POTENTIAL: Depends on what you sell.

SEASONAL: Depends on what you sell.

LICENSE REQUIRED: Not usually, unless you sell something like investments, real estate, or other regulated commodities.

LEGAL CONSIDERATIONS: Depends on what you sell.

SAFETY CONSIDERATIONS: Depends on what you sell.

LOCAL REGULATIONS: Depends on what you sell.

STARTUP COSTS: None.

STARTUP NEEDS: The company you represent should provide you with everything you need to represent them. Assuming you need to be onsite, you'll need transportation to the sales location.

SKILLS NEEDED: Richard's success and comfort level are due to his familiarity with the industry and his passion for the products. I could not do what he does because I don't understand music or musical instruments. Richard can make the piano sing. He can talk to moms and dads about piano lessons. He can talk shop with his prospects, providing essential details about each piano, and talk about the different aspects of music. You need product or industry expertise as well as passion. Sales training would be helpful but you might get that on the job.

MARKETING / SALES NEEDS: The piano store is Richard's sole client. If you have more than one client, they should be in different industries or different locations. You don't want to sell something representing one of your clients at an event, and represent the competitor's product the next day. Once you secure a client, whom you represent as if you were their employee, it's just a matter of aligning your schedule to meet their needs. To get that one client, research prospects in the industry, and then approach them with a proposal. It might be abnormal for them to enter into this type of a relationship, but if you can substantiate your expertise and your ability to be an effective salesperson, they might take a chance on you.

Seamstress

During my high school years, my mom spent hours sewing embroidery on sweatshirts. Working out of a spare room in the basement, she produced the pieces for a lady who sold them at the local farmers' market. Because Mom got paid by the piece, she quickly learned the faster she sewed, the more money she made. Though I didn't appreciate her skills at the time, my mother was a master seamstress.

Fortunately, my sister also learned to sew. She set up a separate sewing room that is covered floor-to-ceiling with sewing equipment and supplies. Her specialty is blankets and quilts for babies and special occasions. She sells her products at local fairs as well as through her website.

My mom and my sister have made good money using their sewing skills.

Do you know how to sew? Are you the person who made your own prom dress, creative tops or pants in high school? Nowadays, sewing your own clothes almost seems like an underground movement. I never thought those skills could become a vehicle for earning money.

When I asked my mom about her experiences, she explained, "Sewing is really broad, and can cover a lot of services and products. It can include mending, tailoring, crafting, embroidery, custom clothing, quilting, drapery making, upholstery, or specialty items."

My mom's client did the selling. That means Mom could focus on fulfilling orders without spending time on other tasks associated with direct selling such as marketing, selling, and collecting money from customers. Some people simply want to do their job and not worry about the other aspects of a consumer business.

A common mistake entrepreneurs make is how to price products and services. My mom says, "Price your product reasonably, but don't under price. You deserve to get paid for the product and for your skill, time and effort. With craft items, people think they can just make it themselves but most of the time they don't! Make a quality product and improve your skills as you go. You'll know if you have priced too high by the reaction you get, but calculate your time into the price. Otherwise, you are not getting paid and will be out of business soon."

In contrast to my mom's model, my sister's clients are all over the world. Some find her through word of mouth, some purchase blankets from her exhibits at local fairs, and others find her products online. Like my mom, she has leveraged her free time, ambition, and skills into a lucrative business that helps her family and is personally and financially rewarding.

INSPIRED BY: Karyn Alba and Kista Marker, QuiltsByKista.com.

EARNING POTENTIAL: Hundreds to thousands per month.

SEASONAL: No, although some seasons/holidays result in increased orders.

LICENSE REQUIRED: No.

LEGAL CONSIDERATIONS: My mom says, "Be aware of copyright restrictions such as licensed art like Disney pictures and other images from movies."

SAFETY CONSIDERATIONS: You might get a needle prick once in a while. Discipline yourself to practice good posture if you are at the sewing machine for hours at a time. My mom says, "Sewing is sedentary. Be sure you exercise, and watch what and how much you eat."

LOCAL REGULATIONS: None.

STARTUP COSTS: Less than one hundred dollars, if you already have a good sewing machine.

STARTUP NEEDS: If you don't have the right sewing machine, expect to spend hundreds for this essential tool. Other than that, your first job could pay for supplies you need to get started. Kista bought everything she needed for about $300, including the sewing machine and notions.

SKILLS NEEDED: You need to know how to sew and be able to learn new techniques. You will need a high attention to detail and patience since you could spend a lot of time on one blanket or article.

MARKETING / SALES NEEDS: Most of your business will come through word of mouth or sites like Etsy.com, where there is a lot of global competition. Focus on finding a niche where your products would be in demand so you can charge a premium. My mom says, "You are responsible for finding your own venue. Search for craft fairs. The good venues can be costly. You want an indoor venue with lots of foot traffic that's popular with vendors. Look for speaking opportunities to show off your product or speak about related topics to highlight your business. Opportunities to share your business are everywhere, from doctors' offices to conversations in line at the grocery store. Look into specialty shops and consignment shops."

Blogger

The blogging Alternative is similar to having a website with affiliate links but it is different enough to merit its own write up. Blogs are special because they require continual updates, where specialty websites don't. There are plenty of examples of personal blogs on the Internet, usually falling under various categories such as mommy blogs, military wives blogs, consultant blogs, project management blogs, foodie blogs, design blogs, and landscaping blogs. There are more than 100 million blogs, with new ones starting daily. Some of these 100 million blogs are "splogs," or spam blogs. Many blogs are lame, uninteresting, not updated, offensive, or something else that would preclude them from getting readers or advertisers.

A very small percentage of blogs make any money, and the list of blogs that make their owners a lot of money is even shorter. I read an article about Heather Armstrong estimating the annual revenue from her blog, dooce.com, is somewhere between $500,000 and $1 million. Isn't that amazing? With a big blog readership and her following on Twitter, she is being recognized by companies anxious to get in front of her audience.

Heather built her business by writing about her life in an interesting and engaging style. It's not uncommon for her blog posts to receive over one hundred comments. The most commented post I saw on her blog was when she was giving away an Xbox. She had over 40,000 comments on that post!* Heather has been ranked as one of the top bloggers in the world. She has written more than 5,000 blog posts and covers topics like breast milk pumps, golf cart rides with Norah Jones, and guys she's dated. Her blog name, Dooce, has become the term used when a blogger gets fired resulting because of something they posted on their own blog.

Ree Drummand, also known as Pioneer Woman (ThePioneerWoman.com), has built a terrific business around her blog. What does she write about? Her life! She writes about cooking, being married to a cowboy, living on a ranch, and homeschooling. Her readers love what she writes. They relate to Ree's posts enough to keep reading, and talking about her with their friends. Advertisers have noticed these audiences and pay for advertising on her site. Ree's first cookbook earned over 1,000 reviews on Amazon. Even years after writing the book, it continues to be a best seller.

Heather and Ree write about themselves, their passions, and their lives. They do it well and they've been able to make a living from it. In addition to getting advertising, bloggers can monetize their audiences with books, webinars, teleseminars, informational products, conferences, and other products. If you develop a platform, you should be able to monetize and add more value for your audience.

A very small percentage of blogs make any money, and the list of blogs that make their owners a lot of money is even shorter.

There is room for more really good blogs. Could yours be one of them? Advertisers have been moving their dollars to online advertising. Maybe your blog could grab a piece of that very big pie.

INSPIRED BY: Heather Armstrong, Ree Drummond, and many others.

EARNING POTENTIAL: At least a few bucks a day, with virtually no ceiling.

SEASONAL: No.

LICENSE REQUIRED: No.

LEGAL CONSIDERATIONS: Incorporate.

SAFETY CONSIDERATIONS: None.

LOCAL REGULATIONS: None.

STARTUP COSTS: Zero to a few hundred dollars.

STARTUP NEEDS: You need access to a computer and the Internet. You could reduce your costs by using your local library. There could be development costs for the blog if you want to get fancy, but you could start without hiring anyone. Make sure you buy your own domain name (like JasonAlba.com) which usually costs around ten dollars annually.

SKILLS NEEDED: Bloggers learn to write well as they write more. You should be disciplined enough to keep producing content. You will need to hone your marketing skills to reach readers and attract advertisers. You should continue to learn about search engine optimization, linking in and out, and other tactics to get people to read and share your blog posts.

MARKETING / SALES NEEDS: To bring in more readers, you need to build a fan base that spreads the word. Your readership might grow through word of mouth rather than search results. Get other bloggers to write about and link to your blog and specific posts. You want people talking about you on Facebook, Twitter, Pinterest, and other social media sites. When the time comes, you'll get to work and negotiate with advertisers.

*http://www.dooce.com/2008/06/30/my-hearts-beating-rabbit

Virtual Assistant

Many years ago, I was on an email list with about 8,000 people, including Kathie Thomas in Australia. Sharing ideas and tips, Kathie frequently contributed to the list. She had created an amazing business helping people become virtual assistants. What I learned from Kathie, and from other virtual assistants, is that you can build a terrific business that accommodates your schedule while earning a solid income. You can do this while choosing the tasks you want to do and the people with whom you want to work.

Let's explore those statements:

Accommodates Your Schedule: Generally, the work is not rush work so you can schedule it around your life. If you choose to work from home, you can do it at nine in the evening or six in the morning, or before or after that movie you want to see. You get the work done when it needs to be done, and you're not tied to a desk eight hours a day. Kathie says, "You choose the hours you work!"

Earns a Solid Income: You can charge what the market will bear. If your client is a small startup in a small town, they might think they can get you for ten dollars an hour. A client in a big city might pay you more than forty dollars an hour. Position yourself and your strengths to charge more. Figure out what you could or should make based on your skills and value proposition. Don't let a prospect talk you down to what they think they would pay a low-skilled person. Respect what you bring to the relationship! Kathie advises, "Doing your homework before you start your business will help you remain on track and know what you need to charge."

Choosing the Tasks You Want to Do: If you like accounting and finances, focus on that as your primary service. If you like editing and writing, focus on that. You don't have to offer every service to your clients. Let them know your strengths and what you want to do, and help them understand what you are not good at or not interested in doing. Kathie says, "You can always refer clients to other virtual assistants when they want something you can't, don't, or won't do."

This is one of my favorite Alternatives because so many job seekers I meet have the skills to do this, and there is a great opportunity to create a recurring revenue stream with their existing network.

Working with People You Like: We've all had to work with people we didn't like. Since this is your own business, if you continually have problems with clients, fire them! You should have fun working in your own business without feeling trapped. It is your right to say, "You know, this just isn't working out," and then have a short conversation where you quit, fire, break up, or otherwise end the relationship.

What does it mean to be a virtual assistant? Basically, you find someone who needs help with their business and office tasks, and you help them without going into their office. Kathie lists the following as some possible services a virtual assistant might do: word processing, data entry, transcription, writing, proofreading, editing, bookkeeping, organizing, scheduling, purchasing, and customer support. And the list goes on. Your competition will inevitably be low-cost offshore solutions. That's okay. Embrace that competition. You can even outsource to them. In other words, if you charge thirty dollars an hour for your work and find some overseas virtual assistants you trust, you can make a profit by paying them six to ten dollars an hour. If you need to lower your rates because of the overseas competition, figure out how to position yourself so that you can justify charging five or ten times what they charge.

There are dozens of resources on what virtual assistants do, how to become one, and how to start a virtual assistant business. This is one of my favorite Alternatives because so many job seekers I meet have the skills to do this, and there is a great opportunity to create a recurring revenue stream with their existing network.

INSPIRED BY: Kathie Thomas, VACoachingClub.com and vadirectory.net/blog.

EARNING POTENTIAL: Twelve to sixty dollars plus per hour.

SEASONAL: No.

LICENSE REQUIRED: No.

LEGAL CONSIDERATIONS: Check with your attorney about setting up the right entity.

SAFETY CONSIDERATIONS: Since you'll likely work from home, there shouldn't be any issues.

LOCAL REGULATIONS: You should obtain a state or city business license. Check with your city.

STARTUP COSTS: Less than one hundred dollars, assuming you have a computer and high speed Internet, which you will be able to write off on your taxes.

STARTUP NEEDS: You will need a computer and phone service. You'll have to set up a convenient payment system for your clients. Kathie says that a decent desk and ergonomic chair are crucial because you will spend hours at your workstation.

SKILLS NEEDED: You should have enough sales skills to find new clients and close sales. Don't neglect your bedside manner, since being unfriendly might lead to a short relationship. Your clients want to enjoy working with you. Being organized is essential. You'll need to be self-directed and able to work by yourself for long periods of time. Flexibility is helpful for meeting the occasional tight deadline. Kathie warns, "Some virtual assistants experience feelings of isolation or depression. Make sure you do your networking away from the office."

She adds, “The biggest mistake people make thinking they can be a virtual assistant is that they just need a computer and an Internet connection. This is not correct. Virtual assistants, by nature, come from an administrative, secretarial or corporate background. They must be very good on the computer with the services they provide, i.e. word processing, data entry, transcription. Also, they must be good at dealing with people. If you're planning to become a virtual assistant, make sure you align yourself with someone who has a network, or a leader who has been in the industry more than five years. Remember that many businesses fail in the first five years so you need a guide or mentor who has made it beyond that barrier.”

MARKETING / SALES NEEDS: Understand your brand and differentiation. You might consider focusing on niche clients such as executives, small businesses, real estate agents, or attorneys. Consult your local chamber of commerce to find out who’s doing what in your town. Read the business journal and check Craigslist for administrative assistant opportunities. You are trying to build a roster of business clients who need your skills.

Newsletter/Writer Distributor

Have you ever subscribed to an email newsletter? I bet you have. Have you ever unsubscribed from an email newsletter? I do it regularly!

Would you pay for a newsletter subscription? I never thought I would, but I do! I pay for a premium subscription to the weekly newsletter published by Randy Cassingham called "This Is True," containing funny, real stories pulled from the news. It's really fun to read. I was on his free list for years and finally decided to pay twenty-four dollars annually for his premium newsletter, which has no advertisements and more stories. Randy's revenue comes from advertisers as well as subscriber upgrades. I've even advertised in the newsletter two or three times.

Could you create a newsletter business, like Randy's? He's a craftsman at what he does because he injects his personality into the newsletters. You feel like you're reading something from a real, normal person. His newsletter is brilliant because it's full of entertaining content and personality.

What interesting topics could you write about that people would want to read regularly? Could it be the stock market? There are a lot of day traders out there trying to game the system. Maybe you have some entertaining insight on parenting? How about your take on housework?

Here's a subject I would pay to read about: lawn and garden. I want an email telling me when I should fertilize, what kind of fertilizer to put down, when to water and when to cover my plants so they aren't destroyed by cold weather. Other advice in this newsletter might include recommendations on what I should plant and when to plant. Is it time to plant pumpkin seeds? What kind of late summer crop should I plant, and when should I do it? If I had a weekly email telling me what I need to do this week, and what to plan for in the next couple of weeks, I would be in heaven!

I am not a master gardener. I'm willing to do the work but I need someone to guide me on the when and the what! Could you help me with that? I would pay you for the guidance.

If you had a successful newsletter, you know who else would pay you? Advertisers. If you had a thousand subscribers, your newsletter would represent a valuable advertising channel to companies. Potential advertisers could include a national company advertising a product relevant to your list. It might be the local store seeking new fertilizer customers, or a small lawn care service company.

You might make more money from advertisers than by reader upgrades. Your strategy could be providing free content to attract more readers, which should lead to more advertising revenue. Or, you can focus just on the upgrades. Either direction requires a different marketing and selling strategy.

Don't limit your reading audience to people at home. Your perfect audience might be a business-to-business audience! Tap into your passion and expertise to figure out what knowledge or consistent message you can provide that would help people.

INSPIRED BY: Randy Cassinham, ThisIsTrue.com. Nicolene Peck, TeachingSelfGovernment.com. Marla Cilley, Flylady.net.

EARNING POTENTIAL: How much you earn generally depends on the number of subscribers. You might be able to count on a few hundred dollars each month. Randy says, "VERY successful newsletter publishers can get into six figures."

SEASONAL: No.

LICENSE REQUIRED: No.

LEGAL CONSIDERATIONS: Incorporate.

SAFETY CONSIDERATIONS: Make sure you don't recommend anything that could be dangerous. Include the appropriate disclaimers in each of your newsletters.

LOCAL REGULATIONS: None.

STARTUP COSTS: None.

STARTUP NEEDS: You need newsletter list software. You can choose a free tool, like Yahoo Groups or Google Groups, or choose from a variety of other tools including paid systems like iContact, Constant Contact, or AWeber. Beware of limitations with free services such as restrictions on charging for upgrades or having paid advertisers.

SKILLS NEEDED: Randy says, "The ability to write well is critically important. Spelling, grammar, and correct punctuation all count. If the newsletter is hard to read, people won't read it. So much of what's online is total garbage. Try reading YouTube video comments! When you write well, your efforts stand out as high quality." Also, you need the discipline to create content frequently, which Randy says is the "absolute key" to success in this type of business. He advises, "The right frequency is probably weekly, or every other week at a minimum." You'll need marketing skills to attract subscribers and advertisers. Finally, you'll learn a lot about spam and spam filters. Randy has become such an expert at dealing with email spam filters that he has written a primer about it at SpamPrimer.com.

MARKETING / SALES NEEDS: To build a subscriber list, you need to get subscribers and encourage those readers to tell their friends who will tell their friends. When you have enough subscribers, you will get to work and negotiate with advertisers.

SEARCH ENGINE OPTIMIZER

Search Engine Optimization (SEO) consultants help clients raise their websites to the top of search results when someone searches for certain keywords or phrases in a search engine. For example, if someone searches for "job search organizer" or "relationship manager," I want JibberJobber.com to be one of the top results, or at least on the first page. An SEO consultant would help me do that.

Sharon Odom has built her business helping companies place higher in search results. Though her business has evolved to include other products and services around business growth and marketing, it started when she became a freelance SEO consultant. From large companies to small one-person startups, everyone who has a web presence would benefit from SEO services. SEO is hard to keep up with since it is very technical and the rules continue to change. This means many businesses should outsource this specialized skill rather than try to stay current in-house.

An exciting aspect of this business is the way your revenue could be structured. In contrast to a business where you sell something once to a client, you could sign long-term contracts with clients who will pay you a monthly retainer ranging from hundreds to thousands of dollars per month. Once you sign enough customers, you can maintain a comfortable business without spending much time trying to make that next sale.

An SEO business is not for everyone. It could be difficult for someone who doesn't like sitting in front of the computer for hours, working alone, or continually learning SEO trends. However, this can be a rewarding business if you are comfortable working alone with technology and can lock in clients.

SEO work is not all about sitting alone in front of a computer. You can outsource much of the work. Sharon shares some success tips, "The hardest part of getting started in SEO is getting clients, mainly because they don't understand what SEO is, how it works, or why they need it. You have to take the time to educate them. Also, it takes a while to generate organic traffic, so they have to understand that they won't see results immediately. From the beginning, you have to manage client expectations and send regular reports in language they can understand. For example, you want to show how many leads were generated and how many sales those leads generated. If you are sending plenty of traffic but it's not converting, they are not going to be happy even though you've done what you promised. It's really about making sure you're sending traffic to a direct response website designed to convert traffic into leads or sales."

Sharon continues, "Outsource as much grunt work as possible, such as content development and link building. Also, hire a virtual assistant as soon as possible, so you can focus on getting clients, staying abreast of technology, and building your own lead generation websites. As an SEO expert, the next step is using your expertise to generate traffic toward sites you own, monetizing those sites with advertisements and sponsorships, and selling leads and services to small business owners."

Sharon shares some pitfalls she has seen in SEO businesses:

- Competing on price. Someone will always be cheaper.
- Not specializing in a particular niche. It is okay to try different niches when you first start, but when you focus on a niche, you become the expert and can command higher prices than a generalist.
- Not specializing. Everyone thinks their business is different and requires a specialist to understand their problems. Become the specialist, learn the language, and get paid more. This creates

value in your own business because you can develop materials once, then slightly alter or customize them for other customers.
- Not developing your own web properties. When you provide SEO services at a fixed rate, you are exchanging hours for dollars. Why not use that same expertise for your own benefit? Build authority sites, get them ranked, and then monetize them. Do the work once and keep getting paid. Again, you can outsource almost all of this.

I asked Sharon how she differentiates her SEO business from her competition and she replied, "Proof. You must show you have gotten good rankings for a competitive term, not some obscure keyword phrase that's never been searched. If you don't have customers yet, show your own properties at the top of the search engines for competitive terms. Anybody can claim to be an SEO expert, but the proof is in the rankings. If you have client success stories and your clients have given you permission, put their testimonials on your website."

Sharon continues, "It also helps if you are in the same city and can meet with business owners in person. Because they are constantly bombarded by calls, emails, and letters from self-proclaimed SEO experts, business owners end up confused and wary. Even though they need the help, they don't know who to trust. Being able to meet face to face will help overcome the trust barrier. You're a real person, not some anonymous voice from who knows where."

INSPIRED BY: Sharon E. Odom, SharonOdom.com.

EARNING POTENTIAL: Hundreds to thousands per client, per month.

SEASONAL: No.

LICENSE REQUIRED: No.

LEGAL CONSIDERATIONS: None.

SAFETY CONSIDERATIONS: None.

LOCAL REGULATIONS: None.

STARTUP COSTS: None.

STARTUP NEEDS: You'll need a good computer and an Internet connection. Most of your work will be online, searching, researching, and implementing. It's all keyboard work. You can meet with clients, but it's not necessary.

SKILLS NEEDED: SEO is an ever changing, moving target. Google has called the shots for many years, but good SEO consultants know nuances of other search engines. As an SEO professional, expect to spend many hours studying changes and trends. The fix you provided last month might be outdated next month, meaning your clients will continue to need you.

MARKETING / SALES NEEDS: When SEO got hot, many Internet "experts" jumped on the bandwagon. Because the barriers to entry were low, anyone could declare themselves an SEO expert. Differentiate yourself from the others because the market is massive. Any website that wants more visitors is a prospect. From big companies to small startups, SEO has become a need for survival. Focus on word-of-mouth referrals and networking within your target audience. Help people understand the value you offer that they won't get from other SEO "experts."

GHOSTWRITER

Professional ghostwriters write for others, on their behalf and in their name. Since we are taught in school to do our own work and not plagiarize, this might seem weird. However, ghostwriting is a very common practice, and is not cheating or plagiarizing. Ghostwriters write entire books on behalf of people you would recognize like Hillary Clinton and Tom Clancy. Ghostwriters can write blog posts, articles for companies or bloggers, and even songs! If you can write, and have a passion for learning, this could be a good Alternative for you.

When you ghostwrite for someone, you are responsible for writing what they would have written in their voice. You become them. You share their message. Ghostwriters are hired when a client does not have the time or talent to write on their own. They might have a busy schedule or an imminent deadline. Ghostwriters might be hired because a celebrity is much better at acting and looking good than writing. Whether you are writing a novel, a memoir or a blog post, take special care to represent the client appropriately.

Bloggers might hire a ghostwriter to keep up with an aggressive writing schedule. It is easy to let a blog get outdated, and companies will pay money for frequent updates. Because this is different than writing a novel or memoir, the compensation is different. If you are paid to write blog posts, you could write discrete and different posts month after month, for years. If you are commissioned to ghostwrite for Tom Clancy, you need to immerse yourself in his works and write as he would have written. Compensation is based on final project delivery, not on monthly recurring deadlines the way a blog ghostwriter would be paid.

I know people who ghostwrite blog posts for a very small per-word fee. Essentially, they are paid to provide a certain quantity of content, and they have to produce the content quickly to earn a decent hourly wage. Quality content isn't a big concern since the objective is frequently updated material for search engines. You'll have to decide whether you are pumping out frequent content for search engines, or if you are more interested in quality writing for human consumption.

When I've considered past ghostwriting opportunities, I have been more interested in contributing to a long-term strategy by partnering with the client. I bid by the project, not by the hour or word count. My hourly earnings usually worked out to more than $200 an hour.

If you can write, and have a passion for learning, this could be a good Alternative for you.

If you win a ghostwriting contract for a book, your fees could be in the tens to hundreds of thousands of dollars. Hillary Clinton's ghostwriter earned a purported $500,000, but that is very, very high. It is not uncommon for ghostwriters to earn tens of thousands of dollars for books, though. Ghostwriting can be financially rewarding and personally fulfilling.

I found Karen Cole, a professional ghostwriter with a team of ghostwriters, at RainbowWriting.com. Her website contains great information about how ghostwriters work, current rates, services offered, and the potential of where your work as a ghostwriter could go. You could offer ghostwriting services on your own, or become a subcontractor to a company like Karen's.

I asked Karen how someone starts a ghostwriting business. She said, "You need to become published online under your own name before you can become a ghostwriter. Then it would help you to land a few jobs on bidding sites like Guru.com or Freelancer.com. The jobs won't pay a lot at first, but you'll build ghostwriting experience. Once you have some references and credentials, start your own ghostwriter's website for search engine optimization so that prospective clients can find you."

She continues, "The most common pitfall is thinking there is something illegal or 'wrong' about ghost writing. It isn't a matter of writing everything for a client and then their name is listed and credited for the work instead of yours. The client does most of the background work and at least supplies the main ideas. The ghost writer is a 'work for hire' worker who supplies the professional writing skills to enhance the client's writing. It's totally legal and aboveboard. If people don't have the skills, the time or the inclination to write professionally, they can still present a top quality book, speech, manual or presentation. The other pitfall may be thinking that you can make lots of lots of money at ghost writing from the get go. It usually takes several years of gaining experience for a ghost writer to begin making 'real money' at the work."

INSPIRED BY: Karen Kole, RainbowWriting.com.

EARNING POTENTIAL: At least ten dollars per hour, to hundreds or tens of thousands per project.

SEASONAL: No.

LICENSE REQUIRED: No.

LEGAL CONSIDERATIONS: Consult an attorney about ghostwriting for regulated industries, like pharmaceuticals, where you might make claims that are illegal.

SAFETY CONSIDERATIONS: None.

LOCAL REGULATIONS: None.

STARTUP COSTS: None.

STARTUP NEEDS: You just need a computer and the Internet.

SKILLS NEEDED: You should be proficient at writing and researching, as well as editing and proofreading.

MARKETING / SALES NEEDS: Your clients will likely be businesses of all sizes. Be prepared to market your services to target businesses and publishers. Describe the value you provide and be ready to share a portfolio of your work. If you sign on as a ghostwriter for established companies that offer those services, you might not need to market yourself, since the company would find clients and send you projects.

PROFESSIONAL RESUME WRITER

I have many friends who are certified professional resume writers. Some struggle to make enough money, some do okay and others do very, very well. How did they get started? Did they major in resume writing in school?

Stories of resume writers who started a few decades ago are fun to hear. The stories include tales of manual typewriters and interesting work conditions, like renting a desk from a small business owner. Now, resume writers have nice computers, work from home, and make their own schedules. Some realized they were so good at marketing resume services that they needed to outsource the actual writing so they could focus on attracting new clients.

Professional resume writer Julie Walraven shares this, "To be successful as a professional resume writer, you should have a strong desire to help people. Too many times people see this as a business to make money and forget that their job is to provide hope and change lives. For me, the success stories of my clients are what fuel me. Just the act of deciding to work with me lifts the weight off my clients' shoulders. Other writers may not have this reason for writing but for me, if I can touch someone's life and make it better, give them hope, and renew their joy in living, my job is done. This has happened many times during my thirty years in the industry."

During recessions, resume writers seem to pop up all over the place. Many newcomers offer services for free or at ridiculously low rates while they build their business. As the economy improves, they go back to what they used to do and leave the industry. People who are good at one thing, like recruiting, shift their focus when the economy changes, and then go back to their comfort zone with another economic change. If you've had a sour experience with a resume writer before, it could be that you didn't work with an experienced, professional resume writer.

What do professional resume writers have in common? As Julie notes, they are passionate about helping others, and they have a high attention to detail. Resume writers are much more than glorified typists. They stay up on current job search and hiring trends, while helping clients position themselves for interviews and job leads. They value the freedom of scheduling their own time and learn how to advertise their own services effectively.

The resume writers I know pride themselves in their craft and use tools like Microsoft Word at an advanced level. They are serious about their value proposition and get as much fulfillment out of a client's new job as they got from getting paid to write the resume. This business can be highly rewarding regardless of how much time is spent or how many clients you have. There is a lot of competition out there but there is plenty of room if you bring excellence and strong marketing to your role.

Do you want to be a successful resume writer? Julie advises, "Today's successful resume writer is more than a resume writer. They understand the need for social media marketing for their clients in the job search and are adept at teaching networking skills. They use those same skills to market their own business, along with the strong content marketing tactics they teach to their clients."

INSPIRED BY: Julie Walraven, DesignResumes.com, and the hundreds of resume writers I've met over the years.

EARNING POTENTIAL: $20,000 annually to more than six figures.

SEASONAL: No.

LICENSE REQUIRED: No, but many certifications are available.

LEGAL CONSIDERATIONS: Incorporate.

SAFETY CONSIDERATIONS: Julie says, "If you plan to have clients come to your home, a business liability insurance policy is a good idea in case someone is injured on your property."

LOCAL REGULATIONS: According to Julie, "Signage is generally not allowed in residential areas. If clients are coming to your home, make sure you learn the rules about signage."

STARTUP COSTS: None, assuming you already have a good computer.

STARTUP NEEDS: Julie adds, "You'll need a computer, office equipment, desk, lighting and other furniture. This could run $3,000 to $5,000, if you don't have it. Creative use of home items can minimize the costs. Off-site data storage as well as storage for hard copies is a common practice. Good virus protection is essential."

SKILLS NEEDED: You should have strong typing, grammar, spelling, and research skills. Julie adds these skills: writing, interviewing, empathy, and analytical abilities to be able to ask questions and pull accomplishments out of the client's mind.

MARKETING / SALES NEEDS: Many people think they can write resumes for themselves. You'll need to communicate why your price of $200, or $700, or $1,500 is worth it to your prospect. Define a particular niche like students, executives, or military personnel and market to them on and offline. Consider marketing to outplacement firms that don't offer resume writing, or companies undergoing layoffs that might contract with you on behalf of their terminated employees.

EDITOR/PROOFREADER

Over the years, I've worked with many editors on my various projects, including multiple editions of my first two books. A good editor understands grammar and punctuation, colloquialisms and exceptions to the rules. I know some of you grammar nerds reading this book have already found a few things that have driven you nuts, or made you think less of me! What's the impact of an improperly edited document? It could lose you a sale. It could lose you a job offer. It could keep you from getting into your school of choice. It could embarrass you, your company, and maybe even your family. It could be a laughing matter, or it could be devastating. Search online for "worst grammar mistakes" and you'll find some funny and embarrassing stuff. Poor editing can negatively impact how the message is received. If your reader gets stuck on an incorrect word or punctuation, they lose focus on the message you are trying to communicate.

Is there a market for editing or proofreading services? Definitely. I'm writing multiple books and I need editors. How many kids applying for scholarships or submitting applications to universities need editing or proofreading services? What about businesses that regularly produce a variety of documents? A lot of authors need their manuscripts reviewed. There are plenty of opportunities to offer these services, and you can get some of this business if people know about you and you are branded appropriately.

There are a lot of people competing in this space. If you are interested in editing or proofreading, I encourage you to get proper training, take classes, and look for certifications. Having the right training and knowing methodologies can boost your confidence and give you a competitive advantage. Certifications and training become your credentials and show a higher level of professionalism and dedication.

Darlene Michaelis, owner of Trailblazing Writing Services, offers the following, "Do your research using the Internet. Find other editors, writers and proofreaders who are doing what you want to do and connect with them. I've gotten a lot of referral business from other service providers whose schedules were full." Advertising only goes so far. Build the awareness that a client's written material will have more impact if it's edited properly by you.

This business can be a lucrative one but understand you must build the momentum and reputation project by project. Getting your name out on the Internet through social media, especially LinkedIn and Facebook, and forging strong relationships is the first step. The exact amount you'll earn is entirely up to you. If you're already providing business communication writing services, then it makes sense to add the editing and proofreading to expand your earning potential. The clients to whom you offer editing and proofreading could become bigger clients if you offer other services, like writing marketing copy.

Darlene shares, "A fellow writer once told me if you're a good writer, you can be a good editor. It starts with a solid understanding of sentence structure and content flow. The key element is maintaining the writer's voice, style, and tone. If you stay true to the author, you'll be successful."

INSPIRED BY: The editors with whom I've worked, and the editors who have offered their services to me.

EARNING POTENTIAL: The prices vary. Some editors charge a flat fee, depending on the scope of the project. Others charge by the hour, starting at around fifty dollars. And some editors still charge by the word, usually around two dollars per word.

SEASONAL: No.

LICENSE REQUIRED: No.

LEGAL CONSIDERATIONS: Incorporate.

SAFETY CONSIDERATIONS: None.

LOCAL REGULATIONS: None.

STARTUP COSTS: Zero to $1,000.

STARTUP NEEDS: You need a computer and an Internet connection. You can edit on free cloud services, like Google Drive, but I find I always come back to Microsoft Word because of the Track Changes features. Good websites for reference include GrammarGirl.com and Thesaurus.com. The Chicago Manual of Style is a very popular reference book for writing professionals.

SKILLS NEEDED: You should have a passion for words, writing, and grammar. Your ability to pay attention to detail will be critical.

MARKETING / SALES NEEDS: Network with your prospects online and at networking events. Be where they are, gain their trust, and help them understand your value (and what they miss if they don't hire you). You need to communicate your value proposition well since there are so many others who say they are editors. Do you clean up the manuscript, or do you help their final product get results? If you are really good, and merit compensation, help your prospects understand why.

Webinar Producer

When a company can motivate its target customers to tune into a useful or interesting topic for five or more minutes, it can be a great brand booster and lead generator.

I do a lot of webinars and video recordings for JibberJobber and other companies. When I work with the company owner on a video, the project can go okay. When I work with someone who specializes in webinar production, things go much smoother. In this scenario, the company hires a production specialist because the management knows if the final outcome is done well, more people will pay attention. If the final outcome is not professional, the company can lose the audience, the opportunity to build a relationship, potential sales, and the chance to create buzz about their company or products.

It is worth the time and money to make sure the webinar recording goes well. Outsourcing this to a specialist makes a lot of sense for companies that want to focus on the core business. Learning the ins and outs of video production is too technical and overwhelming for many people. That is where Shelley Ryan of KillerWebinars.com comes in.

I met Shelley when she worked at a marketing company that hired me for content production. Shelley was the producer assigned to work with me in conducting online presentations. After she left that company, she started her own business to help other companies make well-branded webinars and videos. She is a master at what she does and her clients trust her to take care of all the details involved in producing a polished, finished product.

Shelley deals with a lot of multi-faceted details, including managing subject matter experts like me, who are doing the presentation. Some of the things Shelley handles include:

- **The Content:** Is the guest expert providing the right information in a compelling style?
- **Deadlines:** The expert must make time for more than the webinar itself. Deadlines include content reviews, a technical rehearsal, follow-up on parts that need to be re-recorded, and other tasks.
- **Brand Consistency:** If the product is a series with multiple experts, each speaker needs to stay within presentation guidelines and learn to not pitch their own products.

Then there are the technology and customer support issues. What programs should be used to create and deliver the content? What if there is a problem with audio? Is the presentation being recorded? What if the recipient can't see or hear the speaker? Who is going to do the editing, and where will it be hosted for on-demand viewing? This is too much for many companies to figure out, which means there is opportunity for you to help them.

If you love helping companies get a brand or message out, have an aptitude for technology and graphic design, and can coordinate complex projects, this might be a great business for you.

INSPIRED BY: Shelley Ryan, KillerWebinars.com.

EARNING POTENTIAL: Hundreds to thousands of dollars per project.

SEASONAL: No.

LICENSE REQUIRED: No.

LEGAL CONSIDERATIONS: Incorporate.

SAFETY CONSIDERATIONS: None.

LOCAL REGULATIONS: None.

STARTUP COSTS: $500 to $1,000 or more if you don't already have a powerful computer and a fast Internet connection.

STARTUP NEEDS: Shelley says, "You'll need an account with a web conferencing platform (Adobe Connect, Citrix, WebEx), software for pre- and post-production (Camtasia, Sony Vegas, Adobe Captivate), and a high-end USB headset with a microphone." She also recommends an uninterruptable power supply (UPS) with a 60-minute battery backup so you can continue broadcasting if your power goes out.

SKILLS NEEDED: Between dealing with people and technology, you'll need a lot of patience. As you work with people and deadlines, you will do a lot of project management. You will have a lot of technology know how and will continue to learn and master the software you use. Negotiation skills will help you win new projects, which can easily be bid in the tens of thousands of dollars. Beware of scope creep on your projects and price your projects appropriately!

MARKETING / SALES NEEDS: Your customers will likely be companies, where the need is massive and budgets are allocated. Webinars are a popular alternative to onsite meetings since video-associated costs are much lower than flying people around the country, and a recording can be available forever. Help companies understand the value of this type of marketing, training and communication. If you define your niche and position your services well, and differentiate yourself from other professionals who provide these services, you should be able to communicate the value of using your services instead of your competitors.

Website Content Writer & Link Affiliate

I'm so excited about this idea! In fact, this is one of the ideas that inspired me to begin this book!

After a speaking presentation in northern Virginia, an attendee from the audience thanked me for my presentation. During our conversation, I learned her specialty was writing advertising copy for travel advertising in magazines. I'm sure you've seen travel advertisements in many popular magazines. I asked her if she had thought about making her own website and putting ads on it. To my surprise, she asked, "What do you mean?" She had never heard of people making money doing this.

I suggested she set up a website for people who might be researching vacationing in Jamaica. She would write engaging content for people planning a vacation to Jamaica. She would then put links from Google, Commission Junction, or any other service selling advertising links, on her website, and earn money each time a reader clicked on any of those links.

If she made twenty cents per click, she would only need five clicks to make a buck a day. Five clicks seems doable, doesn't it? I asked if she could build similar websites, like sites for visiting Costa Rica, Puerto Rico, and other popular vacation destinations. She could use the same code and similar content for each website she owned. If she made a dollar a day from each site, the earning potential could be substantial.

The simple formula for this Alternative is CONTENT + EYEBALLS (visitors to your site) + CLICKS ON ADS = REVENUE. Each part of the formula requires work and creativity. Though many try to create an income stream by doing something like this, they give up. It is a simple formula but it takes work to set up and continue to make money. Professional affiliate marketers who make a lot of money have to keep up with the continual changes in search engine techniques. Because competition is abundant, this isn't necessarily an easy business. But it can be a great way to earn money. If you get good at it, you can earn a very good living.

A friend of mine once told me the advertisements on his website make his car payment every month. That sounded pretty good to me! Can you imagine having a website that provides you with regular royalty checks?

I've wanted to do this for my varied interests such as pets (a huge market), or insurance (where I would allow people to rant and complain, and ultimately find other insurance providers). If I had the insurance website with a forum, I could possibly attract insurance agents, brokers or companies as advertisers. For now, I've limited my pay-per-click advertisements to the sites on which I actively work.

Can you imagine having a website that provides you with regular royalty checks?

There is plenty of opportunity for someone to earn good money. Identify niches where you can fill the gaps that would pay well. If you can do well in one niche, you might be able to duplicate your efforts into other niches.

INSPIRED BY: Someone who heard me speak in Virginia.

EARNING POTENTIAL: Hundreds to thousands of dollars per day.

SEASONAL: No, although you can have different websites that specialize in topics that are seasonal.

LICENSE REQUIRED: No.

LEGAL CONSIDERATIONS: Incorporate.

SAFETY CONSIDERATIONS: None.

LOCAL REGULATIONS: None.

STARTUP COSTS: Zero to a few hundred.

STARTUP NEEDS: You need enough knowledge about websites to build a website, write the content, and place the ads. You'll need time to navigate the learning curve. Buy the domain names (like VisitJamaicaRightNow.com) for each website you set up.

SKILLS NEEDED: You need to know enough about website design, writing and search engine optimization (SEO) skills to get started. Perhaps the most critical factor in your success is driving people to your website, which means you'll have to be creative and stay on top of search engine news and changes in online marketing.

MARKETING / SALES NEEDS: To drive visitors to your site, you need to understand how people find websites, what search phrases they use, and what they find when they search for certain phrases. Also, ad placement will have a significant impact on how many clicks you get. Getting visitors to your site, and enticing those visitors to click the links, is what this Alternative is all about.

YouTube Video Producer

The first time I watched my wife use YouTube to learn how to do something instead of doing a Google search, I was shocked. I never thought of going to YouTube to learn how to do things before trying Google or any search engine. As I asked around, I found YouTube is a first choice for many people who want to see how something is done, instead of reading step-by-step instructions.

Did you know if you put a video on YouTube that "catches on," or goes viral, you can make money? That's exactly what Darius Safani is doing. Darius has a YouTube channel teaching video gamers how to get better at certain games. Darius has identified a topic he loves and there is an audience for his topic. He creates the video, edits it, pushes it to YouTube (which is his distribution channel), and works to make it easier for his audience to find the videos.

How do you choose a topic that could produce revenue? Darius shares, "You need to know the content people are looking for and how to display it in a way that differentiates your video from everyone else's. The games I play appeal to people close to my age. My audience prefers to watch videos made by someone close to their age."

Creating something funny, edgy or interesting that will go viral is not easy. Many companies spend thousands of dollars trying to figure this out. Google "how to make a viral video," and you read a lot of speculation on how to do this.

Some people who have created popular videos get paid as their videos become more popular. For example, something as mundane as "how to tie a tie" is one of the top searches on YouTube. Seriously! Look it up! Look for videos on how to apply makeup or how to braid hair, both popular topics. You don't have to be funny, break something, or experience a death-defying moment for your popular video to earn money.

YouTube wants you to be successful in this business. Darius says, "YouTube created a handbook that lists ways to engage the audience and explains how long each step takes, on average, from creating a video to engaging your audience, getting comments and subscribers, to using YouTube Analytics. If you are doing "vlogs" (video blog), post right before there is an event related to your video (like a new video game release). More people will be searching for the event making it more likely they will find your video. Making videos relevant to what people search for is key."

Darius continues, "It is important to know there is a difference between ad revenue and being in a partnership. Ad revenue may come from just one video. In a partnership, ads will appear on all your videos. You also get the ability to choose the types of ads on your videos, special customization, and branding options for the channel such as video and channel banners."

There's an opportunity here, and the barrier to entry is relatively low. However, Darius says, "It is not as easy as it looks. A lot of people are trying to do this. You can't expect people to find your video just because you posted it. Make the best quality videos you can. If you don't, you are relying on luck for people to find your video. YouTube shows the videos with the most views first which is why quality counts. If your video is interesting or cool, others will share it. This is how videos go viral. No one will share a poor quality video."

Darius' strategy is to post new videos frequently, which is different than the one-hit wonders like Charlie getting his finger bit. Frequency is key to Darius' model. He says, "Inconsistent uploading is a big mistake. You can't have a consistent fan base if you don't consistently upload new videos."

How much time does this business take? Darius says, "It can be time-consuming because I upload every day. I spend an hour recording every two days, and thirty to sixty minutes editing each day. It doesn't feel like a lot of work because I enjoy doing it."

Can you capture your expertise, no matter how mundane it might seem to you, that will help millions of others solve their problem? If you can, you might be able to create a revenue stream.

INSPIRED BY: Darius Safani, YouTube.com/user/glem3.

EARNING POTENTIAL: Hundreds to thousands each month.

SEASONAL: Depends on your topics.

LICENSE REQUIRED: No.

LEGAL CONSIDERATIONS: Incorporate.

SAFETY CONSIDERATIONS: None.

LOCAL REGULATIONS: None.

STARTUP COSTS: None.

STARTUP NEEDS: A great idea, and a video camera or screen capture software.

SKILLS NEEDED: Based on what I see in many videos, you don't even need presentation skills. Some are funny because the presentation is not polished. If you are serious about this Alternative, create a strategy. Plan your topics and content. Learn about video editing. I have found this task to be the most time consuming. It might make sense for you to outsource the video editing piece while you focus on the content creation and marketing.

MARKETING / SALES NEEDS: Your topic and how you present it are the most important things for marketing. There are some things you can do to increase shares of your videos, but success has more to do with how others talk about your videos than how you market them (as proven by some well-financed marketing campaigns from big companies that don't go anywhere). As they say, "Content is king." Refer to the YouTube handbook. To learn tactics and techniques for increasing your video viewership, find stories and case studies of videos that have gone viral.

Drop Shipper

Can you imagine selling a mundane product, like floor mats, as your next big career move? Probably not. Erika Wilde didn't imagine she would be doing it either, but she does, and she does quite well.

Erika does not have a warehouse of mats waiting for shipment. She focuses on what's called "drop shipping," where you set up an online storefront, receive orders, and then pass those orders to a company that fulfills (packages and ships) them. As a drop shipper, you focus on marketing and sales, and use another company to complete the order.

Drop shipping is a brilliant idea. A friend of mine co-founded Doba.com, a site that provides the right tools for those who want to get into the drop-shipping business. You set up a storefront (a website, not a brick-and-mortar store), and then pass sales to other companies that fulfill the order. There's no inventory or shipping, allowing you to focus on attracting new customers.

I know it's not as simple as that. It takes work to grow a drop shipping business, but it definitely can be done. Erika says, "To be successful in this kind of business, you need to treat it like a real job in the sense that it runs best when worked on daily. But it is a job that I CAN leave dormant and ignore for awhile because it basically runs itself. If I neglect it for too long, though, things get ugly. It's good to work every day on the business, even if just for an hour."

Customer service can be tricky. Erika cautions, "When I first started, I didn't figure out discounts and the return policy. If I got a pushy customer on the phone, I would sometimes give too much of a discount. Or, I would change the return policy from customer to customer. It cost me money and time. I learned to get my policies in writing and stick to them."

Erika shares how she made her role less critical to the business' success, which is a challenge many entrepreneurs face. "Over time," she says, "My business has become less dependent on ME. I have an awesome employee who has been working for me for four years. I have taught her how to do just about everything in the business. I have put this in writing as well. It's almost as if I were writing a franchise manual for my business. Now I feel like I could walk away from the business, and my employee or another owner could take over. At the beginning, I used to joke with my husband that if I dropped dead, the business would also drop dead. He would have orders coming in and no clue what to do with them! That is no longer the case."

I read a story in a magazine about a kid who went to a local factory that made car floor mats and found they had a surplus they wanted to eliminate. He ended selling them online for a high profit. This wasn't drop shipping, but it is an example of how you can focus on ONE product and make it work.

Whether it comes from a company's surplus or from one of Doba's partners, find a product to sell, and then connect with customers. Erika is able to offer many different floor mat sizes and styles through her partnerships, without the hassle of running a warehouse. This allows her to focus on Internet marketing, which is critical for this type of business. To learn more, check out the free resources at Doba.com.

INSPIRED BY: Erika Wilde, StopDirt.com and Jeremy Hanks, Doba.com.

EARNING POTENTIAL: Thousands per month.

SEASONAL: Different products can be seasonal, but there is no limit to the number of products you can sell.

LICENSE REQUIRED: No.

LEGAL CONSIDERATIONS: Incorporate.

SAFETY CONSIDERATIONS: There shouldn't be any since this will typically be an Internet storefront.

LOCAL REGULATIONS: None.

STARTUP COSTS: Spend whatever it takes to get your website up and running. You should be able to establish a hosting account for less than ten dollars per month. If you go through a service provider like Doba, you will pay a monthly fee.

STARTUP NEEDS: You'll need knowledge and the ability to market on the Internet. A good-looking website with checkout processes that customers trust enough to place an order is crucial. If you are passionate or knowledgeable about what you are selling, you will be more valuable to your customers.

SKILLS NEEDED: Writing (advertising copy, blog posts, and other content), learning and researching the ever-changing world of online marketing are essential. You should be able to identify market trends and conduct competitive intelligence research. Customer service skills are a must.

MARKETING / SALES NEEDS: Depending on what you sell, it can be a crowded space. You'll need to excel at Internet marketing and learn all you can about buying advertising, search engine optimization, and other facets of Internet marketing. Continually conduct competitive intelligence research to gauge how your competition is doing, and learn what you can do better. Ask your customers for referrals and to spread the word about your website.

Beekeeper

Professional speaker Brad Barton once gave me a unique thank you gift. It was a small bear-shaped container filled with honey his kids gathered from their bee hives. I thought it was a clever representation of his brand and it definitely sparked a conversation that helped people remember him.

Brad and his family are kind of nuts about honey. They have studied beekeeping and are involved in local beekeeping groups. Though they operate on a small scale, they are very serious about their honey operations. I asked Brad how much money he could make selling honey. He said, "If you have forty hives, which isn't very many, you could easily earn $15,000 a year. You'll work about three days a month to make that."

Wow! Work three days a month to make over $1,000 a month? That's over $300 for each day of work. You could earn enough money to pay bills, catch up on credit cards, pay rent, and even make house payments. That sounds good to me!

Wow! Work three days a month to make over a thousand dollars a month? That sounds good to me!

To get to where Brad and his family are takes a lot of work. How do you obtain forty hives? How do you keep the bees alive? How do you prepare the honey for sale? Who buys the honey?

There is definitely a learning curve with beekeeping. Challenges abound, including colony collapse disorder and predatory insects. In fact, during the last twenty years, the number of colonies in the United States has shrunk from about seven million to just over two million.

Brad's teenage daughter, Aubrey, runs the family beekeeping business, making sure the bees are healthy and producing and everything is in order. She suggests reading Beekeeping for Dummies, commonly used as a beginner's textbook for beekeepers. She also advises finding a mentor with a successful track record from the local beekeeping club. Because there will be challenges and solutions unique to your geographic location, learning the skill from someone who keeps bees in your area is vital.

Here are tips from the Bartons, "One plus One equals Success. Always start with at least two hives. The liability of beginning this fun hobby with one hive is that if your bees do really well the first year, you will think you're a good beekeeper. Believe us, you're not. However, if your bees do poorly, you will think you're a terrible beekeeper. Most likely, you're not that either. Beginning with two hives gives you a much better chance of building a strong colony and perhaps a weak one. You'll stay encouraged and humble at the same time.

Selling your honey is as easy as letting neighbors and friends know you are open for business. Your local, wild, raw honey will be so much more delicious than anything they can buy at the grocery store and they will happily pay a premium price. Our family gives dozens of half pound bear gifts to neighbors through the Christmas holiday. We include a note that some of that honey came from their own backyard flowers and vegetables. We receive a plethora of orders around the holiday from neighbors who want more of their very own backyard honey to give as gifts to friends, family and employees. Also, displaying at craft fairs and farmers markets makes for a fun and lucrative Saturday morning. Bring the kids. Your honey sells even better with youngsters in the equation."

Brad continues, "While neighbor kids make $2.75 in an afternoon at a lemonade stand, my kids often sell $180 worth of honey from their front yard honey stand in a three-hour stretch. Tell me this isn't a kid's dream come true! They supply an in-demand product to passers by while padding their bank accounts as they learn about hard work, margins, and cost of goods sold. How cool is that?"

In addition to making money, this is an Alternative that will help you keep your local plants and trees healthy and producing. It's a win for you, your neighbors and your community.

INSPIRED BY: Brad and Aubrey Barton.

EARNING POTENTIAL: $1,000 or more per month, depending on the number of hives.

SEASONAL: Yes. Brad says, "Bees do not go dormant or hibernate. They cluster in the winter and convert their honey stores to heat so the hive temperature stays at 92.5 degrees all winter long. The queen still lays, albeit at a much reduced rate, and they get by on shivers until the spring build up. Because there isn't much to do in the apiary, you'll have several hands off months."

LICENSE REQUIRED: Check with your city.

LEGAL CONSIDERATIONS: Check local honey production and sales regulations.

SAFETY CONSIDERATIONS: Aside from the obvious, like an occasional sting, you are dealing with hive health, moving equipment or hives, handling food, and working with live creatures. There are no shortcuts to getting the right equipment and training. If you are allergic to bee stings, this isn't an Alternative you should consider. Brad says, "We keep an EpiPen in our medicine cabinet in case a neighbor has a strong reaction."

LOCAL REGULATIONS: Don't expect to put forty beehives in your neighborhood, although you may be able to find homes for hives around the community. Brad says that each state has different licensing requirements. In Utah, there is a ten dollar annual fee that enables you to sell at craft fairs and farmers markets. "Because honey is gathered instead of being processed," continues Brad, "There are no FDA food handling permit requirements that I'm aware of in Utah." He advises checking your local government's rules on beekeeping. Brad learned that Ogden City's beekeeping restrictions fall under the nuisance ordinance which basically means that he keeps bees in city limits at his neighbors' implied consent. However, one complaint call from a neighbor and his apiary has to go.

STARTUP COSTS: Less than $500. Brad says, "If you start with two hives and you don't want to bother building your own, you'll be into it about $250 for the hive equipment. Safety equipment is going to set you back another hundred dollars or so. An extractor can be borrowed or rented."

STARTUP NEEDS: You will need beehives, a suit, equipment for collecting honey, equipment for storing and selling honey, and of course, the bees!

SKILLS NEEDED: Bees are living creatures. You are taking on the responsibility of preparing a safe environment for them and maintaining that environment. Learn about bees and the signs of hive health. Hive maintenance cannot be neglected. Take care of the hive and the product (honey), package it well, and you could have a great business.

MARKETING / SALES NEEDS: Brad's kids know they can make extra money quickly by selling small containers door to door in their neighborhood. What if they got local stores, including health foods and grocery chains, to sell this "locally produced" honey? With the right marketing, and networking with the right people, they could take advantage of the trend to buy local, organic products. These would be excellent repeat customers. Choose a handful of ideal target markets and then make a marketing/sales plan for each market.

Custom Artwork Producer

I met Greg Olsen, a famous Christian painter, when he was exhibiting at a Costco one evening. I told him about this book and asked to interview him because of the business and income he has built with his skills and passion. During our conversation, he told me about his daughter who doesn't paint but she's really good with pencil art. She has financed holiday gift shopping through commissioned artwork.

Earning a commission means you get paid to create custom art for someone. It may be as simple as being paid fifty to $150 to create a pencil rendition from a photograph. Or it could be something significantly more complex and lucrative. For example, some of the great works you've seen by Picasso, da Vinci and other artists were commissioned.

There is something special about having a one-of-a-kind, custom-ordered piece of art. Commissioned art could be cherished for generations. If you have artistic talent, try earning money by creating and selling art. Like Greg's daughter, it could be an income stream that could supplement the family budget. Or, like Greg, it could turn into a financially successful business, and become your primary income.

Some artists use their skills to draw holiday window paintings and children's bedroom murals. I knew a girl in high school who painted pictures on storefront windows. Because she was very talented, she was able to make more money than her friends who worked minimum wage jobs. And, she got the satisfaction of seeing her artwork each time she passed the window. Another friend hired an artist to paint her daughter's bedroom with princesses and scenes from favorite movies. How you create and deliver your art varies, depending on your skills and who appreciates your work.

Greg shares ideas on how to create a strong revenue stream as an artist, "If you really want to be successful doing this, you'll need to get the word out! Make flyers with examples of your work and ask art supply stores or boutiques to post them. Use social media to show photos and the resulting art pieces inspired by them. Focus on depicting good likenesses since that is what most clients are really looking for. Be creative. Don't just copy a photo! Try inventing unique backgrounds or combining photos into an interesting montage. This gives the client something beyond just a snapshot that is more interesting than a photo. Ask for referrals from clients because word of mouth is great advertising."

As a business owner, learning from mistakes is critical. Greg shares, "My biggest mistake was not giving enough time and energy to market. Make a good product and then find ways to let people know about it!" If you don't spend time marketing your product or service, who will?

You can find inspirational stories and examples of other artists and how they make money on sites like Etsy.com. Look at their styles, products and pricing, but don't limit yourself to Etsy as a distribution channel. If you contact customers directly, instead of waiting for them to find you online, you might attract more long-term and higher-priced customers.

INSPIRED BY: Greg Olsen, GregOlsen.com.

EARNING POTENTIAL: Highly variable. Consider charging by the project instead of by the hour.

SEASONAL: No. Art can be given as gifts for holidays or special events like a housewarming or birth of a child. Solicit store owners to paint seasonal window displays.

LICENSE REQUIRED: No.

LEGAL CONSIDERATIONS: None.

SAFETY CONSIDERATIONS: Depends on your medium.

LOCAL REGULATIONS: None.

STARTUP COSTS: Less than $200.

STARTUP NEEDS: You'll know what supplies and tools you need to make your creations. You might need a quiet and peaceful place to work where you can store your work in progress and your tools.

SKILLS NEEDED: You must have artistic ability. You will learn business skills including estimating projects, billing and collections. Many artists love art but dislike the business side. To maintain a profitable venture, get really good at the business side.

MARKETING / SALES NEEDS: Identify your market. Are they individuals or businesses? Network, showcase your work, and ask for referrals. You'll probably grow your business more through word of mouth than any other strategy.

Custom Candy Maker

Peggy Hunter has a sweet business – she makes candy. You can tell she is passionate about her business producing custom, made-to-order chocolate truffles and solid chocolate designs. Candy making has been around forever, although it seems to be more of an underground hobby than a common way to make money.

There are candy artisans who make money on the side, creating their confections for fun and intrigue more than for a business. Some figure out the business side, specifically marketing and sales, and earn a lot of money. For example, Jerry Swain started making "chocolate balls" while he was in college and now distributes his chocolates through Costco.

Peggy's candy shell is made out of dark, milk, or white Guittard chocolate. The gouache centers of each truffle are made fresh with heavy whipping cream, Belgium dark, milk or white chocolate. Every piece is decorated with edible, colorful, flavorless luster dust, and each candy is individually bagged and labeled, and placed in organza gift bags or boxes, depending on the size of the order.

She explains, "I make molded chocolate truffles and the designs are unlimited. I love making specialty gifts for people's fiftieth birthday celebrations, chess sets for NASA engineers, and horse truffle suckers for horse enthusiasts. I have hundreds of additional molds available for baby showers, wedding favors, sports, birthdays, hobbies, every holiday, and special events."

Clearly, Peggy is serious about her candy business. The different molds help her market into a variety of specialty occasions and celebrations. She has learned how to use a variety of ingredients and takes pride in how she presents her final product. As a business owner, I would love to send specialty chocolates to my clients who can appreciate the taste and wonder about the custom design.

Since everyone knows what chocolate is, this is a business that your family can help you build. Peggy says, "I ship to family for holidays, weddings and birthdays." Naturally, her family shares the chocolates and her contact information with businesses. "I sent 450 horse truffle suckers to a Missouri business owned by a friend of a cousin who ordered them for VIP clients. I developed a standing order with a company for all the holidays. The company gave the candy to select customers and employees."

Could this turn into something more for Peggy? As Jerry did, she could work with distributors like Costco to expand her reach. Or, she could keep her business at a local level. Peggy says, "I would love to have my own store and sell supplies, make candy, and teach classes."

This might be an Alternative where your relatives think you are crazy, but this is a multi-billion dollar industry. Perhaps there is room for your unique ideas and recipes.

INSPIRED BY: Peggy Hunter, who started her business during her job search. Facebook.com/pages/Totally-Truffles-and-Treats/107715599299190.

EARNING POTENTIAL: Hundreds to thousands per month.

SEASONAL: Peggy says, "This is not seasonal. I make candy all year for all occasions. Christmas is the busiest holiday but Easter, Valentine's Day, and even the Chinese New Year are very busy."

LICENSE REQUIRED: Yes. Because you are preparing food for sale, you need to have a business license and follow all government regulations for food preparation. Investigate what you need to do and have your documentation in place.

LEGAL CONSIDERATIONS: Incorporate.

SAFETY CONSIDERATIONS: Since you are making food, you need to be very careful. You don't want to get publicity for food poisoning! Peggy states, "I am very, very careful. My kitchen, molds, the cooking utensils and pots are all sanitized before I begin. And I have a separate refrigerator for all my candy supplies." Consider renting a commercial kitchen for your production.

LOCAL REGULATIONS: Check with your city.

STARTUP COSTS: About $350, assuming you have access to a commercial kitchen.

STARTUP NEEDS: You'll need general kitchen and specialty candy tools, including the molds.

SKILLS NEEDED: You should know your way around the kitchen and be ready to market, sell, and fulfill all orders. Peggy adds that you need to have "passion!!!" And, practice makes perfect! She has been making candy for fifteen years and definitely has improved since her first sale. Take a class, watch videos on YouTube, and rent instructional videos. Practice and try new ideas. Watch what the candy industry trends are. Peggy visits candy stores to compare her products against theirs and get new ideas.

MARKETING / SALES NEEDS: You could probably develop a nice revenue stream from local clients, starting with friends and family. Encourage word-of-mouth advertising. Make it easy for people to talk about you by giving them cards or flyers they can share with others. If you want to ship your goods, develop a social marketing strategy and ask your friends and followers to spread the word online. Peggy shares some sales ideas, "Throw home parties with other crafters. Advertise new designs and special events. Make cards to place in orders and give to people. Keep mailing lists and send flyers during the holidays. Make and give out samples."

*http://www.costcoconnection.com/connection/
201302?pg=22#pg22.

Garage Sale Reseller

I love driving through busy neighborhoods and passing houses that have garage sales every weekend. Most people host garage sales (also known as yard sales) to get rid of stuff they don't want anymore but they think the things are too good to throw away. One person's junk is another person's treasure, right? Garage sales are usually popular during the spring and summer months. Selling stuff professionally is different than the casual, once-a-year event to get rid of your stuff. Professional garage sellers make money by selling from a key location, usually the front yard, where there is a lot of traffic. Why not take advantage of a great location?

On my way toward the city center, going out of my town, I regularly pass a house that holds a garage sale every weekend. Since it is on a busy road, everyone knows about it and people are always browsing to see if there are any interesting items. A close neighbor, Emily Slimak, uses a different tactic. She finds seasonal things and sells them during the appropriate seasons. For example, throughout the year, she strategically hunts for Halloween costumes and then sells them during the two months before Halloween. She organizes the costumes so they are easy to pick through and uses the same clothing racks you would see at a clothing store for a professional presentation.

Emily also finds merchandise at other garage sales that she buys and then resells online. She says, "Buyers at a garage sale are different than online shoppers. Garage sale buyers want a bargain and will always try to talk the price down. That's their mode. Online buyers, however, are looking for something specific, and aren't necessarily focused on haggling about price."

This business takes a lot of time. You have to be available to do it during peak sales times like weekends. You have to figure out where to get your merchandise. If you underestimate the amount of time and planning that goes into acquiring merchandise for resale, you'll probably fail at this business. Do you have the time and energy to look for stuff you can resell for a profit? Are you willing to spend hours sitting in front of your house waiting for customers? Do you live in an area where you would get a lot of visitors? If so, maybe this can be a great business.

Emily shares valuable insight to help you be successful with this business, "You need room to store the items you buy. I have considered renting a storage unit for items because they can overtake the garage quickly, especially if you don't turn them over fast enough."

She adds, "Become familiar with the value of things you want to buy. A smartphone is a great tool for looking up an item to check its original or current retail value on the spot. If the asking price is too high, or too close to the original price, you won't have much room to mark it up. If an item has several parts, make sure all the parts are there. Also, when buying baby and children items, make sure the products have not been recalled."

Emily continues, "I don't like buying items that sellers claim to be in good working condition only to get them home and find they are not. This makes them not sellable. After getting burned a few times, I have learned to carry a screwdriver and batteries in my purse to test before I buy. Be prepared to deal with people who will waste your time by setting appointments to get an item and then never contact you again. Decide if you feel comfortable having people pick up at your home, or if you would rather meet them at a public location."

INSPIRED BY: Emily Slimak.

EARNING POTENTIAL: More than $1,000 per month.

SEASONAL: Garage sales are usually open during nice weather. Reselling online can happen anytime.

LICENSE REQUIRED: Check with your city.

LEGAL CONSIDERATIONS: Incorporate.

SAFETY CONSIDERATIONS: This can be a physical business. You will be lifting, setting up, cleaning, moving around, and having others on your property. Keep the environment safe for your buyers. Check with your insurance agent to make sure you are properly covered.

LOCAL REGULATIONS: Check with your city.

STARTUP COSTS: Less than one hundred dollars.

STARTUP NEEDS: You should have tables, although many garage sales will display products on the grass or driveway. You'll need inventory, which means you have to figure out where to get merchandise to resell. Signage and advertising is critical. Plan to spend a lot of time working in this business.

SKILLS NEEDED: You need to be able to deal with the public regularly. You will become expert in finding inventory and pricing the items appropriately to make a profit. You will learn advanced negotiating skills because garage sale buyers are experts at negotiating.

MARKETING / SALES NEEDS: Typically, your clientele will not be repeat customers. Focus on advertising to passersby, which means having good signs on streets and corners. Check local regulations for signage requirements. Post online in the garage sale classifieds section. You don't need to market to companies, unless the company has employees who are your perfect target audience and you want them to know. Facilitate word-of-mouth advertising.

HANDCRAFTED CARD MAKER

Have you ever received a handcrafted thank you card? I've gotten a few of them over the years. Each time I open the handmade envelope, I think, "Wow, they took time to put this together . . . for me!" The card itself makes a powerful impression even before reading what the sender wrote.

In our microwave-quick, I-want-it-now world, taking the time to do something personal and special can make a significant impression. Jane Ann Hart, who also works as a professional meeting planner, has a passion for creating personalized cards with a strong impact. She has the time, a good eye, and the attention to detail you'd expect from someone who creates high-touch pieces of art. And, she puts her passion for photography to good use by decorating the cards with photographs she has taken.

Jane Ann's passions and skills come together nicely to create a revenue stream. Most people won't fret over paying three to seven dollars for a store-bought card. Jane Ann's designs and photographs make her cards personalized works of art. She can easily make a few hundred dollars a month doing something she likes to do in her spare time. How many cards would she need to sell to generate a significant income?

If she sells one hundred cards at four dollars each, she makes an easy $400, minus expenses. If she got a rush order for 300 cards, could she fill it? It would take a lot of work. It's okay to keep her business small, but if Jane Ann wants the business to be her primary income source, she would need the necessary processes and systems in place to maintain that income.

To scale her business, Jane Ann could do various things. She could recruit subcontractors to create and ship the cards, or she could outsource to companies that specialize in design, creation or fulfillment. If she outsources creation and fulfillment, she could focus her time on marketing and sales to get big corporate orders. She could develop relationships with people who do customer outreach to clients and prospects. For example, a chief executive officer's administrative assistant might want to send anywhere from ten to 200 holiday cards each year. A sales professional might want to send personalized cards to prospects and clients. Imagine repeat clients who make bulk orders throughout the year.

Jane Ann shares thoughts on how she handles her business, "There are two aspects of note cards: the creative and the business. These are right and left brain activities. I can only focus on one side at a time, although I enjoy both equally. My camera is always with me and there are many opportunities to take photographs. Editing and formatting the photos are part of the creative process. The business side, including printing, marketing, distribution, tracking sales, expenses and revenue, requires a different skill set and mindset. I literally have two sides to my office – one side devoted to the creative and the other to business."

INSPIRED BY: Jane Ann Hart, jahart.com.

EARNING POTENTIAL: Four dollars or more per card.

SEASONAL: No, although orders could increase during holidays.

LICENSE REQUIRED: No.

LEGAL CONSIDERATIONS: Research copyrights in photos, phrases, logos, and other content.

SAFETY CONSIDERATIONS: None.

LOCAL REGULATIONS: None.

STARTUP COSTS: Less than $200.

STARTUP NEEDS: You need an initial stock of supplies including card stock, glue, pens, and any embellishments for decorating the cards.

SKILLS NEEDED: You should be patient, have an attention to detail, and be interested in crafting. If you want to incorporate photography, you have to own the photos or you will face serious copyright infringement issues. That is why Jane Ann uses her own photos on her cards.

MARKETING / SALES NEEDS: You'll likely grow this business by word of mouth. Ask for bulk orders from companies, sales representatives and account managers who want a high-touch deliverable. Your ideal customer would send a lot of cards but doesn't have the time to create (or write in) them. These customers should give you repeat orders. Make sure you have a web address on every card so the recipient knows where they can place their own orders. You can put effort into search engine optimization but the card space is crowded. You might be more effective marketing through personal relationships than competing online.

Information Product Seller

Do you have expertise in something? Anything? Can you tell or show me how to do something? Do you teach people how to make, think, be, act, or talk? You can't personally go to every client's home or office, but you can record your training so we can access it from a computer, CD player, smart phone, tablet or other device.

I do a lot of training on how to use LinkedIn. When I recorded my LinkedIn training and packaged it on a DVD for my target audience, I filled a need for them. Before my DVD was available, there wasn't a good way for LinkedIn members to get comprehensive, no-nonsense advice and instruction on how to benefit from LinkedIn. The DVD has become a phenomenal revenue stream for me and complements my brand and other revenue streams.

She could make about a $50 margin on each four-pack of CDs she sold.

I sell the LinkedIn DVD when I speak, from my website, through Amazon, and through career professionals and resume writers who are closer to my target audience than I am. Revenue from the DVD plays a significant role in my business, especially when other revenue streams are low.

Creating information products is not a new concept. At a conference I recently attended, I passed the keynote speaker's booth after she delivered her presentation. The audience loved her presentation and a line of conference attendees waited to meet her at her booth. She was selling different self-produced CDs for fifteen dollars each.

By my estimate, it cost about two dollars to produce each CD, which means she would make a thirteen dollar profit on each CD she sold. Her content was distributed over four or five CDs, which means one conference attendee could end up buying sixty dollars of her product. She could make about a fifty dollar margin on each four pack of CDs she sold. If ten conference attendees bought the bundle, she would make an additional $500 at that conference.

Information products work well for non-speakers, too. You can produce your own CDs or DVDs and make as many (or as few) copies as you want. If you think you will sell a lot, outsource disk production to a company that specializes in replication. I have a company that replicates my DVDS and I buy 1,000 DVDs each time I order. It is relatively easy to update content and burn more disks as needed.

The key to this business is providing expertise and training others want. The more exclusive your expertise, the less competition you'll have. Do you have the right expertise to make this business work?

INSPIRED BY: The many professional speakers who taught me about this opportunity, and my own success in selling information products.

EARNING POTENTIAL: Hundreds or thousands per month.

SEASONAL: No.

LICENSE REQUIRED: No.

LEGAL CONSIDERATIONS: Incorporate.

SAFETY CONSIDERATIONS: None.

LOCAL REGULATIONS: None.

STARTUP COSTS: Fifty to $1,000.

STARTUP NEEDS: You need to be able to record your expertise in an audio or video format. You can use a variety of tools to make the recordings including a voice recorder, Camtasia (or a free alternative), a video camera, or other tools. After you edit the content, you can burn a few disks and you are ready to sell. If your market is big enough, and responsive (they buy your stuff), consider replicating the disks to lower your cost of each disk you sell.

SKILLS NEEDED: You need to have a decent presentation and be well organized. Designing content was not as easy as I thought it would be. It took me a few tries to get it right. You might have to script what you say, word for word, like I have done. Additionally, presenting well is not as easy as some people make it look. Consider outsourcing the editing. Once the content is burned on a disk, you've done the easy part. The real challenge is compelling people to pay for it.

MARKETING / SALES NEEDS: As I mentioned earlier, I sell my DVDs from my website, through Amazon, when I speak, and through partners. Each distribution channel requires a different strategy. I've heard of two distinct strategies to sell information products. One strategy is based on your brand as an expert where people readily recognize your name. If you are the expert, they'll want to learn from you. No fluff, just solid content. Grow a fan base who buys your product and market new products to them. The other strategy is to use search engine optimization (SEO). If you have content people want, get it in front of them when they search for it online. If you have optimized your site for the search engines, you'll make sales from people who found you on a search engine but didn't know about you before. They came for the content, not your name.

INVENTOR: OOH LA BRA

I learned about Ooh La Bra from a blog post by Thom Singer.* Thom wrote about a college friend, Lisa Angelos McKenzie, who had an idea for a business. On Thom's blog post, Lisa says, "The bra strap idea was one of those situations where I was sitting around a pool with friends and said, 'Wouldn't it be cool if . . . ?' And the idea was born. The idea is that the bra strap becomes jewelry on the shoulder that's designed to not only be functional, but show in a tasteful and beautiful way. Bra straps that are sexy and practical."

You can see Lisa's products on her website, OohLaBra.com. She carries more than just bra strap bling. Her product line has grown to include related products, which is a natural evolution for her business.

I don't expect you to create a business to compete with Ooh La Bra, which has over eighty styles. However, I hope her story and success encourage you to rethink an idea you already had but didn't think was good enough for a business. Lisa's product is for women's brassieres, which have been around for hundreds of years. Can a novelty product (defined as "being new, original, or unusual") really become a business? Lisa proved that it can.

Don't underestimate your product idea. Lisa's idea solved a problem of which I wasn't aware, but it was a problem her target audience had. Her creativity, background and resourcefulness made her the right person to make this business successful. Lisa says her idea came from sitting around with friends, informally brainstorming. There are still many problems that need to be solved. If you have a solution to a problem that has a big enough market, you might be able to create a profitable business.

An idea isn't enough. I asked Lisa what it takes to move forward, since so many people get stuck in the idea stage. Lisa responds, "I am an idea person. Ideas are constantly swirling around in my head. Every so often, there is an idea I consider a 'no fail' opportunity. Something that excites me so much, it's all I can think about. When this happens, I Google the idea to see if there are other competitors doing something similar. If I find competition, I check out the strengths or weaknesses in their product or concept. Just because someone is doing something similar doesn't mean they will be a threat to your success. It is a big world. The key is being smarter than they are, and making sure your message gets heard."

Lisa continues, "After researching the competition, I run the idea past friends and family and listen to their reactions. I often get additional ideas that enhance the original concept. If I receive a lot of positive feedback, I know I am onto something. Negative feedback would be something like, 'I tried that once and it was boring.' Or, 'I saw that online.' Comments like that usually give me an indication that the idea isn't that unique."

"However," says Lisa, "When I get a lot of positive feedback, the next phase usually takes place on a napkin. I'll be at lunch and the idea is so present in my mind that I start doodling information that helps me work out the idea like a big puzzle. The bottom line is this: STOP talking about it and DO IT. You can be assured it's going to fail if you do nothing. And you'll probably kick yourself when you read about the same idea a year from now, being done by someone else who had the courage to proceed."

To be successful in a business like this, Lisa advises, "Find a supplier who is dependable. Create a price structure that allows you to have a strong retail, wholesale and distributor model. Create brand identity. Develop a loyal following. Put social media to work for you. Offer amazing customer service. Keep growing and developing the product line because customers are always looking for something new. Find mentors who have been in similar businesses who will share tricks of the trade, examples of order forms, and tips on exhibiting at trade markets. These mentors will be an INVALUABLE resource for you."

Lisa cautions people who have great ideas. She writes, "I have friends who have amazing product ideas and they spend so much time getting the product ready for market that they never actually get the product to market. Two years ago, a friend of mine told me about an amazing invention she dreamed up. She spent months on the patent, months on the industrial design, months on the business plan, months working with potential investors, and to this day the product is still being talked about and isn't out to market. She has spent two years of her life on this! Her vision is so big that she might be missing out on getting this started because she is trying to make it perfect from the get go. Put your best idea, product out there and continually modify and adjust until you reach the vision. People can be their own worst handicap by working tirelessly but never seeing any results because they don't pull the trigger."

I asked Lisa about wearing a lot of hats (marketing, overseeing manufacturing, fulfillment, and design). Here's her advice on how to manage it:

- In the beginning, don't feel like you have to hire a full-time staff to operate your company. You probably have friends who are more than happy to have hourly work. Take advantage of those relationships and pay people to do jobs that free your time to grow your company.
- When you work on important things like developing your website and e-commerce store, do your best to not get distracted by Facebook, news updates or random emails. I think idea people are a bit ADD, and it really takes extreme dedication to just focus on the tasks at hand without getting distracted. I am very guilty of that!
- Make a to-do list every day and focus first on the items that bring in money. Then allow time each day to knock off the non-

revenue items. Make sure the first two hours of your day are spent on the income-producing tasks.

INSPIRED BY: Lisa Angelos McKenzie, OohLaBra.com.

EARNING POTENTIAL: Hundreds to thousands per month.

SEASONAL: Depends on your product.

LICENSE REQUIRED: Check with your city.

LEGAL CONSIDERATIONS: Incorporate.

SAFETY CONSIDERATIONS: Depends on your product.

LOCAL REGULATIONS: Depends on your market.

STARTUP COSTS: Depends on your product, manufacturing, design, and patents.

STARTUP NEEDS: Expect to do a lot of research. You will spend more time and money than you planned for product design, manufacturing, and order fulfillment.

SKILLS NEEDED: The skills you need depend on how much you outsource. If you outsource a lot, you will need project management skills. If you don't outsource, you will need skills in design, manufacturing, order fulfillment, marketing, sales, operations, administrative functions, and more.

MARKETING / SALES NEEDS: The marketing strategy for a business like this would include online marketing (SEO and getting affiliates) and traditional marketing, such as speaking, networking and PR. Word-of-mouth endorsements in the right markets will build momentum for your product.

*http://thomsinger.blogspot.com/2011/09/niche-business-shows-its-bra-straps.html

Mail Order Baker

Do you have a killer recipe handed down from past generations, or some wonderful recipe you invented in your own kitchen? I know people with secret recipes for everything from breads to salsas. Because they are convinced they can sell their food, or license the recipe, they won't share the recipe with friends or family.

If this is you, consider going into business like the owners of Anna's Gourmet Goodies. Chris Duke and his family make and sell homemade cookies and brownies to clients throughout the U.S., and to American military bases around the world. Their product line includes their "Artisan Cookies," made with premium ingredients sourced from local farmers.

Is it really possible to create a new, or better, food item? Chris says, "It is possible to carve out a niche market in the specialty foods business. Most states have a specialty foods organization where you can get more information about these businesses. Visit the Specialty Food Association website (specialtyfood.com) to learn more." I found an abundance of inspiration on that website. There are industry contacts, people who are living their dream through creating a business from their recipes, and examples and ideas to expand your mind on what these businesses look like. Visiting the site should give you names of people or companies with whom you should network as well as inspiration to take the first step to start this type of business.

As a business owner who sits at a desk most of the time, I can't imagine taking the time to bake and ship treats for prospects and customers. But I know these products would make a favorable impression. I would gladly pay someone else to make and ship a specialty treat, a very nice high-touch gesture that should help nurture a relationship.

I know it can sound crazy to start a business like this. Run the idea and samples of your food by friends who work at companies that send gifts to clients during the holiday seasons and for other special occasions. A lot of companies do this. Chris says, "Research to find out if your product is something that people and businesses will actually order at a price that makes you a profit. It is okay to ask family and friends, but you also should get feedback from people you don't know. They will be your best source of information as to whether you've got potential for a real business."

Maybe you don't need a special recipe. There might be another key ingredient to a gift food business like this. Chris says, "Don't have a secret recipe? That might be okay. Packaging and marketing are key success factors in any business. If you have an eye for design and can create something memorable people will order, you might just have the recipe for success."

INSPIRED BY: Chris Duke and his family, AnnasGourmetGoodies.com.

EARNING POTENTIAL: $1,000 or more per month.

SEASONAL: Possibly. Sales might increase during holidays, but other celebrations aren't necessarily seasonal.

LICENSE REQUIRED: Chris says it depends on your location. Follow local and state regulations. Contact your local department of agriculture and the health department.

LEGAL CONSIDERATIONS: Chris advises, "Get a good insurance policy to protect you in the event of unforeseen issues with your products. If your products are sold on store shelves, most retailers will want to see proof of insurance."

SAFETY CONSIDERATIONS: Make sure you have all the right licenses for making and selling food. Care and cleanliness can't be understated. You want to be famous for great food, not for making people sick. Chris advises registering your business with the Food & Drug Administration as a part of the Food Safety Modernization Act.

LOCAL REGULATIONS: As this is a highly regulated business, you should use a commercial kitchen or a qualified home kitchen. If you don't have one, check with local restaurants or businesses to see if you can lease or borrow their facilities during their off hours.

STARTUP COSTS: From $2,000 to tens of thousands of dollars.

STARTUP NEEDS: Startup costs can vary depending on whether you buy your own equipment or rent or lease equipment. Budget enough for raw materials. Food costs can vary widely with the season. For example, it is not uncommon for the price of eggs to double during the year. You'll need a facility for manufacturing and office space to run the business. Make sure you have all the licenses and permits. Start off on the right foot to avoid being shut down.

SKILLS NEEDED: Chris says you need kitchen skills along with planning, shopping, budgeting, financial management, marketing, selling, packaging, and shipping skills. Customer service is very important all the time, but especially during startup. As you grow, you can outsource or hire others. In the beginning, you have to know your product or risk losing your market by relying on someone else who may not share your passion. The presentation should be consistent with the price level and market you intend to attract.

MARKETING / SALES NEEDS: You can market this online but you might find more business through talking to local prospects. Try getting word-of-mouth referrals and corporate clients such as salespeople, executives, account managers, and business owners. These customers would become repeat customers by putting your products into their budget. Chris adds that word of mouth will always be the best way to acquire customers.

PROMOTIONAL PRODUCTS SELLER

Fred Behle was in the property management industry while his wife Debbie is a career saleswoman. They got interested in the corporate promotional products arena while investigating business ideas that would allow them to work together. Fred already had some experience in this type of business so they were able to set up their business, with access to tens of thousands of promotional products, fairly quickly.

To access that many products, the Behles researched companies that pool promotional products. Fred and Debbie chose to partner with Advertising Specialty Institute (ASICentral.com). ASI helped them get their business up and running, including a website for clients to place orders and browse the complete catalog online. With ASI's help, the Behles were ready to sell!

I need and appreciate a consultative partner who can help me find the right items quickly and order the right things.

This business is similar to the Drop Shipper Alternative because both businesses resell products from other companies. The key difference is that clients in this business are more likely to make repeat orders since they are businesses buying promotional stuff for conferences, meetings, celebrations, and events.

Why would a corporate client buy through the Behles' business instead of just going online and making an order? When I looked at making purchases for these types of items, I was quickly overwhelmed by the variety of products, pricing and quality. As a corporate customer,

I am too busy with my daily duties running my business. I need and appreciate a consultative partner who can help me find the right items quickly and order the right things. I don't have time to browse and research thousands of options. I want to pick up the phone and ask what the best options are for my situation. I want to know you understand and care about my business. That high-touch service is something I cannot get from search result. I want the personal touch and would rather have you help me than try and figure it out on my own.

In this type of business, providing that personal touch is the great opportunity. I asked Debbie about competition and she said this market is big enough that she's not worried about it. In the end, the winners will be those who provide the right personal touch. There are a lot of companies, big and small, that are prospects for these offerings.

Fred says, "To grow this business, you need to network, network, network. Like any sales job, ask for referrals after you have successfully provided a customer with good products to create successful marketing programs. Help them understand you are not just giving out promotional products. You are creating marketing solutions to help companies grow their business, add new customers, increase sales from existing customers, and retain existing customers."

He adds, "Continue to market and bring in new customers. Don't rely on just a few large accounts. It is a challenging and competitive industry. Focus on customer service and marketing solutions, not just price. We are very selective in choosing our manufacturers. They must provide an excellent product with professionally applied company logos, ensure on-time delivery, and be competitively priced."

INSPIRED BY: Fred and Debbie Behle, MarketingSolutionExperts.com.

EARNING POTENTIAL: Hundreds to thousands of dollars per order.

SEASONAL: No.

LICENSE REQUIRED: No.

LEGAL CONSIDERATIONS: None.

SAFETY CONSIDERATIONS: None.

LOCAL REGULATIONS: None.

STARTUP COSTS: Less than $500.

STARTUP NEEDS: You could start off with a catalog to hand out, but if you follow Fred and Debbie's example, you'll want a website where your customer can place orders.

SKILLS NEEDED: You need to nurture relationships, network, and leverage cold calling skills. You need to be able to manage vendors and resolve customer issues. Submitting bids timely and correctly could significantly impact your business.

MARKETING / SALES NEEDS: Debbie cold called the city offices to ask about an upcoming annual fair and was invited to bid. This seems to be a very fragmented (and confusing) space, with vendors and websites offering many solutions. If you can be more of a solutions provider and consultative partner to your clients, you might be able to find and keep clients better than through competing on price. Focus on establishing high-touch, quality relationships. Plan to spend a lot of time on the phone and networking face to face at events.

Restaurant Discount Seller

When I was a poor newlywed, I had a very small paycheck that I took to the credit union to deposit. As I was standing in line, minding my own business, the guy behind me struck up a conversation. One thing led to another and he introduced me to his boss. Because of this introduction, I started hawking buy-one-get-one-free restaurant cards door to door.

I never thought I would do door-to-door sales, ever. But I quickly learned it could be a great way to make money, both for me and my boss, who directed a team of door-to-door sales representatives canvassing the city.

Before you turn the page to the next Alternative, let me explain why I love this idea. The discount card I'm talking about is not the popular discount coupon book or magazine kids typically sell for school fundraisers. Those books could be an inch thick and offer thousands of dollars in savings. For twenty dollars, those books are a real bargain, aren't they?

I rarely buy them because they contain coupons I would never use. Some discounts are a meager 10 percent while some vendors offer products and services that don't interest me. There are so many pages, you could spend thirty minutes just trying to figure out where you want to go.

This Alternative isn't about a discount book with a lot of deals. Instead, this is a discount card for one specific restaurant. Let's go back to my experience as a newlywed. Tyvan, the owner of the company, had an agreement with two restaurants. One was the best Mexican restaurant in town and the other was a "high end" steak house in a hotel. There was one card for each restaurant, which was part of the brilliance of the business. The card was easy to sell and easy to use. You either liked Mexican food or you didn't. You either liked steakhouses or you didn't. You didn't have to flip through a bunch of coupons wondering how many you would actually use.

A huge selling point was that each card represented significant savings. For example, if you bought the Mexican restaurant card you would get something like two free appetizers, ten buy-one-get-one-free lunches, and five buy-one-get-one-free dinners, all for twenty dollars. Even if you only used it once or twice, it paid for itself.

Even though the price of the card was the same as a big coupon book, it was an easier sale. My pitch was, "Do you like Mexican food?" Or, "Do you like to eat at Eduardos?" If the answer was no, I'd ask if they liked the local steakhouse. I'd show them the cards, show how it paid for itself in the first two visits, and the decision to buy was quick and easy. If the customer questioned whether the card was a scam, I would encourage them to call the restaurant to confirm its validity.

I got half of the sale and Tyvan got the other half, so each card was worth ten dollars to me. If I hustled, I could sell one card per hour. Another sales guy seemed to sell at least ten cards a day. Even though I was a rookie, I could still make more than minimum wage. If I was a better salesman, I could have made a lot more.

To start this business, visit a local restaurant and pitch the idea. Tyvan took care of the design and printing so the restaurant only had to agree to honor the card without paying anything out of pocket. As far as I know, Tyvan did not share the sales revenue with the restaurant. They honored the agreement because it brought in new and repeat customers.

INSPIRED BY: Tyvan Schmitt, TyvansCoupons.com.

EARNING POTENTIAL: Up to twenty dollars per card.

SEASONAL: You can do this year round, although door to door in the winter isn't fun. You would sell to companies during the cold weather.

LICENSE REQUIRED: Check local regulations to see if you need a solicitor's license.

LEGAL CONSIDERATIONS: Incorporate.

SAFETY CONSIDERATIONS: It's fun to walk around a neighborhood but be mindful of private property and dogs! Always be careful about going into homes. You should be able to make the sale and collect payment on the front porch.

LOCAL REGULATIONS: Check with your city.

STARTUP COSTS: Approximately $1,000 for the design, printing, lamination, card holders (like a brochure), and other supplies.

STARTUP NEEDS: You need a legal agreement with the restaurant, and the card design and production. After that, it's all about knocking on doors!

SKILLS NEEDED: Because this is door-to-door sales, you should have thick skin for taking rejection graciously, regardless of how amazing your cards are! You may want to hire a team of experienced sales people, which puts you more in a management role than a sales role. Even if you are managing people, you could still knock doors or visit companies during the day.

MARKETING / SALES NEEDS: The ability to make door-to-door sales and ask for referrals is essential. Getting past the gatekeeper at companies and small businesses could be lucrative because you can sell a lot of cards at one business. One of my colleagues went into businesses and regularly sold a bunch of cards. The more well known or popular the restaurant, the easier the sale.

Tips Booklet Producer

When I travel the country speaking to groups of job seekers, one of my favorite things to tell the audience is that everyone in the room has expertise in something. Some people are experts in their chosen profession while others are experts at working well with people. Some have expertise in negotiations and others are experts in keeping their work area clean and organized.

What is your expertise? In my experience, people have a hard time defining their expertise, perhaps because they think it has to be in what they were trained to do, what their last boss paid them to do, or what they studied in school. They associate a job title or tasks they do in their job with their expertise. Your expertise, and even your passions, might be completely different than a previous job title. To help you figure out your expertise, ask your friends, family or colleagues how they define it? Depending on the source, you'll hear different answers.

I love this Alternative because many people, including you, have expertise but are overwhelmed with the idea of writing a "real" book.

Put together a list of things in which you have expertise or about which you are passionate. Narrow your list to what really excites you and you could find the right topic for a tips booklet. This is a small pamphlet-like book that tells a reader exactly what they need. They can read it quickly without having to sift through too much wording. If you are an expert, others might be interested in learning from you.

Paulette Ensign knows people are interested in learning from an expert, and they will pay to learn from that expert. Paulette has developed a significant business by selling her expertise. Her sixteen-page tips booklet, *110 Ideas for Organizing Your Business Life*, has sold over a million copies. She wrote it in 1991 to make a few more dollars by sharing her knowledge and experience as a professional organizer. Since then, Paulette has built a successful business helping others create tips booklets.

I love this Alternative because many people, including you, have expertise but are overwhelmed with the idea of writing a "real" book. I'm not saying you won't put considerable effort into writing a tips booklet, but I think the task of writing a much shorter booklet seems less overwhelming than writing a 60,000 word book with hundreds of pages. If you wrote a full size book, you would benefit through book sales and brand recognition. A book gives you credibility as an expert. A tips booklet can do the same thing. It can increase your revenue through sales, and play an important role in earning speaking and consulting revenue. As the author of a tips booklet, you should be able to sign new clients and increase product sales revenue. As an author, I've experienced this and I've seen many other authors realize these benefits as well.

INSPIRED BY: Paulette Ensign, TipsBooklets.com and CollectionofExperts.com.

EARNING POTENTIAL: Hundreds to thousands per month.

SEASONAL: No.

LICENSE REQUIRED: No.

LEGAL CONSIDERATIONS: Incorporate. Include language in the booklets that protects you from liability. Put appropriate disclaimers in the booklets and make sure you own all the content. Don't borrow phrases without citing the source.

SAFETY CONSIDERATIONS: None.

LOCAL REGULATIONS: None.

STARTUP COSTS: None.

STARTUP NEEDS: Your passion and subject matter expertise are key. You can easily write a tips booklet with a notepad and a borrowed computer (at the library), which means you can do this with no investment.

SKILLS NEEDED: You will need to be able to organize your thoughts, write, and edit the booklet. Once the booklet is done, you will do a lot of marketing.

MARKETING / SALES NEEDS: There are various ways to market this type of product. Paulette says she has sold over a million copies of her booklet "without spending a penny on advertising."* Where is your target audience and how will they look for and find this information? Is the topic of your booklet written for the average person who will use a search engine, or is it for people in a niche industry? If it is for a specific audience, you could be reviewed in industry magazines or by influential industry bloggers. To generate sales or consulting opportunities, public speaking and attending networking events are great branding tactics in positioning yourself as the expert.

*http://tipsbooklets.com/about.html

LEATHER & VINYL DOCTOR

When I started this book, I decided I would not include franchise opportunities for two reasons. First, the cost to get into many franchises is prohibitive. Second, many franchises have very structured policies and rules that don't allow the franchisee much freedom in making strategic decisions, scheduling, and purchasing product. The purpose of this book is to present low-cost options offering flexibility and customization that will inspire you to act on an idea.

Then I met Aubrey Cramer, co-founder of The Leather & Vinyl Doctor. I asked Aubrey about his franchise opportunity and was amazed to learn there really is a franchise you can get into for a low price. As I learned more, I realized this might be an attractive Alternative. If there is one franchise that is affordable and has the flexibility you want, there must be more.

Aubrey worked for the company in Australia and came to the United States with a business partner to develop franchises. He is passionate about helping people successfully grow their franchise business. In a nutshell, you pay the initial franchise fee, obtain the proper transportation (a van or trailer), and you service customers making leather, vinyl and fabric repairs in your territory. You might fix a leather couch or a car's leather interior. You make the repairs at the customer's location. Or, if it's a large job, you might perform the work in your garage or shop.

Aubrey says his franchisees enjoy a lot of freedom in their schedule and can do very well financially. Coming from a variety of backgrounds, they include a former social worker, a retail sales manager, a student, a boiler maker, an accountant, a marketing manager, and a radio broadcaster.

I was excited to include a franchise opportunity as one of the 51 Alternatives because franchises are kind of a "business in a box." You don't have to create the business from scratch. As a franchisee, you have access to corporate resources and systems that would otherwise be very expensive to create. The franchisor helps you with marketing, training, and everything else you need to be successful.

Gilbert Vasquez, a franchisee, says, "It takes the right attitude and willingness to learn this business model. Be very passionate about your business and your customer will see your enthusiasm. They will believe in you. If you want to be successful, you have to be motivated and open minded. Don't expect business to come to you. There are plenty of opportunities. You just have to go out and look for them."

Janet Sloan, a franchisee in Utah, had this to say, "This franchise gives me complete freedom with my time and future income. It was a good choice for me and my family because the upfront cost was realistic. The Leather & Vinyl Doctor gives us the opportunity to set our goals as high as we want. We really have no bosses dictating what is expected. We are our own bosses and it feels great!"

Is it that easy? It is empowering and exciting, but it's not all easy. Janet says, "The most difficult part of this business is bookkeeping. Keeping track of the income and expenses is hard. It is difficult to keep up with scheduling new clients, free estimates, delivery, pickups, and general appointments."

You have probably investigated franchise opportunities as you researched alternatives to a real job. All the opportunities I found while in my job search were really expensive. Other opportunities are out there. Review them and conduct your due diligence.

INSPIRED BY: Aubrey Cramer, Co-founder, LeatherRepairUtah.com.

EARNING POTENTIAL: Jobs can vary from ninety to $1,200.

SEASONAL: No.

LICENSE REQUIRED: No.

LEGAL CONSIDERATIONS: The franchisor should take care of legal documents, but you should have your own attorney review them before you sign.

SAFETY CONSIDERATIONS: You'll be working in a variety of settings with different types of repairs, tools and chemicals. Heavy lifting might be required, especially if you take furniture to your repair facility. When working in this type of environment, Aubrey advises using common sense.

LOCAL REGULATIONS: Aubrey says, "There shouldn't be any local regulations. All products are non-toxic."

STARTUP COSTS: From $10,000 to $20,000.

STARTUP NEEDS: You'll start with a franchise agreement, which is less than ten thousand dollars, and then you need a trailer or van and other startup materials suggested by the franchisor.

SKILLS NEEDED: You will "own a saleable territory," market, sell, and perform the repairs. You will learn most of the repair skills on the job.

MARKETING / SALES NEEDS: Gilbert says, "A lot of business is self-generated. You have to take time to distribute flyers to homes, detail shops, hospitals, medical facilities, car dealerships and RV facilities." Your customers can be a one-couch client, a multi-piece hospital, or a car dealership. Figure out where your best margin is and focus on that market. Decide whether you're going to target individuals or companies.

Conclusion

Are you inspired?

I hope so. Here are a few things I want to share now that you've been instructed and inspired.

What ideas have you come up with on your own? What stories and advice from the Alternatives triggered your own Alternatives? Share them with me (Jason@JibberJobber.com). Let me know if I can share them with others on 51Alternatives.com or perhaps in a future book on Career Management 3.0.

While thinking about entrepreneurs, I figured out what the steps of a business are. I came up with a circular model that looks like this:

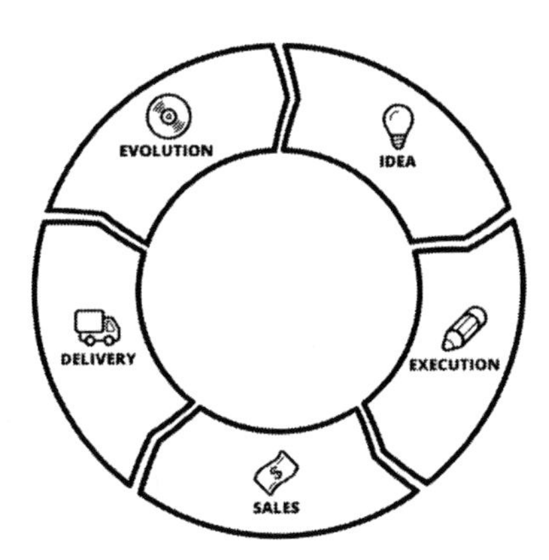

Idea: This is your idea. It could be one of the Alternatives in this book. It could be an idea for a residual product or service, or it could be an idea you had before you picked up this book.

Execution: Ideas are worth nothing unless you take action. Even if you patent the idea and license it, that is still execution. Action, action, action!

Sales: No matter how great your idea is, if you don't make an effort to sell it, you will not make any money.

Delivery: This would be shipping a product or delivering the consulting hour you sold to your client.

Evolution: This is the key to staying alive in business. Based on customer and market feedback, and continual competitive analysis, you should evolve your ideas and offerings by continuously returning to the idea stage.

The first four steps in the cycle were intuitive to me. I didn't realize how important and significant the fifth one would be. Successful evolution means you stay up with, or ahead of, the market. It means you introduce new products and start the cycle all over again. Since I started JibberJobber in 2006, the software has evolved, as has the business plan and pricing model. If I were stuck in my 2006 ideas, without understanding the market and my users, JibberJobber would not be around today.

Rare is the business that can exist on one idea and ride it forever. Get used to the concept that there will be course changes during your business life. They may even be so drastic that what you eventually end selling is completely different than your original idea.

So how do you get started? I thought about writing another section in this book outlining the exact steps, but there are too many variables. Here is a brief set of steps to move forward from here. Flesh them out and modify them as appropriate:

First: Commit yourself to honestly doing your business instead of just trying to do it. It is time to make a commitment and move forward with your resources to make it work.

Second: Talk to people. Get feedback on your ideas. Ask who would be interested and what people like or don't like. Consider their feedback but realize you'll have naysayers. There will be pessimists who are not as dedicated to making it work as you are. If you want to make it work, work at it regardless of the immediate support you get. Make sure the people you ask are qualified to answer honestly. If they aren't prospective customers, they might not be qualified to answer as prospective customers!

Third: Get the right paperwork in place. This includes filing for a business license and opening a business checking account. You may not think it's as tedious as I did, but it's essential for protecting your assets. This is a one-time task that is worth the time and trouble. Once you complete these tasks, you can move on to making money. Next, set up all your tools and startup items, if you can. If you can't, make some sales and use that money to buy what you need. Otherwise, be ready to deliver, whether you manufacture a widget or paint a mural. The sooner you can delight your customer, the sooner they can evangelize your business.

Last: Pick up the phone or send your first email. Now you are looking for sales. Don't sit around waiting for them to come to you. Learn to embrace sales. Many people fear this step, but you can learn to love it. Talk with people, solve their problems, enrich their lives . . . that is what sales is.

These steps will get you started. You'll learn a lot as your business grows. As your offering evolves, you'll tweak things like your prices, your sales pitch, and how you deliver your products or services. But none of that will happen until you start.

Don't overthink this – get started!

Jason Alba
Fellow Entrepreneur